*EVEN
SILENCE
IS
PRAISE*

EVEN SILENCE IS PRAISE

quiet your mind
and awaken your
soul with Christian
meditation

RICK HAMLIN

W PUBLISHING GROUP

AN IMPRINT OF THOMAS NELSON

Published in Nashville, Tennessee, by W Publishing, an imprint of Thomas Nelson.

Thomas Nelson titles may be purchased in bulk for educational, business, fundraising, or sales promotional use. For information, please email SpecialMarkets@ThomasNelson.com.

ISBN 978-0-7852-4459-2 (audiobook)
ISBN 978-0-7852-4447-9 (eBook)
ISBN 978-0-7852-4443-1 (TP)

Library of Congress Cataloging-in-Publication Data

Library of Congress Control Number: 2021947921

Printed in the United States of America

22 23 24 25 26 LSC 10 9 8 7 6 5 4 3 2 1

To my beloveds, known and unknown, whom I have prayed for and who have prayed for me.

Contents

CONTENTS

The Peace That Passes Understanding

What kind of author starts a book with a bunch of apologies? I'm really no expert on prayer—even though I've written several books and countless articles on the subject. I really struggle in my practice of getting silent with God—even though I do it religiously day after day. I leap at the idea of meditation like a dog playing catch—and would be hard-pressed to tell you exactly when I've caught the ball in midair.

I would be foolish enough to say maybe that's you too. We seek the peace that passes understanding. We long to feel the unconditional love that knows no bounds. We struggle to find a habit that makes that possible. And like the apostles and preachers over the centuries, not to mention your third-grade Sunday school teacher, we end up calling on God's mercy again and again.

You know what? That's all for the good. This is a book for beginners, amateurs, like us. Is the topic of this book prayer or is it meditation? Truth to tell, I'm writing about both. There is a great deal of very convincing scientific research about meditation and its profound psychological and physical benefits.[1] The studies are exhaustive and to be taken very seriously. But for me, as a practicing Christian, I can't separate meditation from prayer. Meditation is an essential part of my prayer practice. And *practice*, indeed, is the operative word.

At a dinner with some dear friends, two of them started talking about how they had tried meditation. They'd taken an online course and had read a book. One was a churchgoer; the other was not. One had had a very scary bout with cancer and was still not out of the woods. *Good for him*, I thought. *God knows the meditation surely must help.* But they both confessed they weren't very good at it. They tried it but found it almost too challenging.

"Of course it's hard," I wanted to say. That's why we do it. The silence can be deafening. That's why I keep listening to it. Sometimes the connection seems good—I can feel myself rising on that updraft of the Spirit. Other days I think I'm terrible. My mind casts too many shadows, my overthinking brain working overtime. And yet that's exactly *why* I do it. Don't judge yourself. I don't think Jesus does. It's the publican who stands far off from the temple, looking down, praying with that same sense of failure, "Lord, have mercy," whom Jesus calls out. Not the Pharisee who brags about how great he is. Don't ever feel bad about feeling that you're less than perfect. There can be holiness in that state of humility.

Not long ago I was running up to the park in my busy city neighborhood when I passed a lamppost with an eight-by-ten piece of paper taped to it. I couldn't read it as I passed—not as I was jogging by—but I did notice the word *FBI*. All at once my head went into worry mode, my mind joggled into uncertainty. *There must have been some terrible crime committed in the neighborhood that I don't know about,* I thought. *They're trying to keep it secret from us, but it's so awful the FBI has come in to do an investigation.*

A mob killing, an attack on the subway, an espionage ring exposed, drug trafficking, human trafficking, an illegal gambling bust—I kept imagining countless horrible scenarios. Why else would the FBI be there?

A few days later I was on the same route, doing the morning jog (mind you, I go slow—really slow—especially on those hills), when I saw a wide trailer with multiple doors, electrical cords snaking down the sidewalk, a truck unloading large lights, a caterer cooking breakfast. FBI? They were shooting an episode of the TV series that goes by that name.

Don't blame me for an overactive imagination. I would say that's one of God's gifts—for all of us. Imagining something that *might* happen is a way we prepare ourselves, get ready, do the wise thing. My wife likes to say that if she worries about a thing happening, then it's more likely *not* to happen. I tease her by calling it the Prophylactic Power of Worry. Of course, she was put to the test one year when she gave up worry for Lent and both of our then-college-age sons decided to do a spring break trip to Mexico just when the news was full of horror stories about gang violence south of the border.

Talk about a lesson in humility.

Jesus, as usual, is working on us in multiple ways when he tells us to consider the birds of the air. Do they ever fret as they go about their days? Are they overly anxious? Not exactly. (Not for nothing do we accuse dim folk of being bird-brains.) At the same time, those birds are working constantly, foraging for the next meal and the food they'll feed their children. As do we.

Let's stick with those birds for a minute. Ever watch an eagle fly on the breeze? It doesn't do it by an effortful flapping of its wings (like me pumping my legs and arms as I try to run up a hill). It catches an updraft and rises very naturally. Smoothly. It reminds me of what we can do when we seek and catch the Spirit in silent meditation. We rise through work that is not entirely our own. (I'll say more about birds in chapter 5, in case you're interested.)

We can't be certain of anything in our world—except death and taxes, as the old line goes. But we can be certain of God's love. Love is the opposite of fear. Love is what casts out fear (1 John 4:18).

One of the images that comes again and again in my meditation is the "cloud of witnesses" (Hebrews 12:1). You are one of them. I've never met you. We might possibly meet someday. We might exchange emails or texts. You could remain forever a stranger. But I can picture you and thousands and thousands of others joining us as I close my eyes and sit. I feel myself praying for your needs—even though I don't know what those needs are. I sense you as part of my community. I sense us all, worrying, trembling, distracted, burdened, tired, despairing, wondering what the future might hold. And then holding that promise of love in our hearts, souls, bodies, and minds. Sitting in a silence that speaks volumes.

chapter one

Meditation in Church?

It's a Sunday morning, and I'm walking down Broadway to our church on New York's Upper West Side. On my way I pass one, two, three, maybe four people with mats rolled up under their arms, their bodies clad in Lululemon as they make their way to the yoga studio a block away. There they'll get the usual diet of limbering, stretching, deep breathing, turning themselves into a pretzel—and then that sacred moment, called forth by a teacher with a voice that could disarm a tiger: they sit in silent meditation. Just the thing to calm the nerves in a busy city.

Meditation. It's cool and hip and not at all uncommon. You could bring up the subject at a New York cocktail party, everyone dressed in black, and no one would blink an eye. Many would volunteer to tell you about their own practice. Maybe they've been doing Transcendental Meditation ever since they took a class in it back in the '90s; maybe they have studied Zen and have a teacher they check in with regularly. Maybe they listen to an app on their phones. Maybe they do it on a cushion at home, legs crossed, eyes half-closed. They might even do it at work, where their enlightened employer has a room specifically set apart for mindfulness and scheduled opportunities when employees can check in to check out. It's good for business, too, they say. Increases productivity and creativity.

All the while I think, *Gosh, we in the church really messed up.* Did we ever let these good people know there is a rich

Christian tradition of meditation? Praying in silence, closing out the material world to look to the world beyond, emptying the mind, seeking God in "the cloud of unknowing," as an anonymous English author put it in a fourteenth-century book of that title.[1] Listening for the "still small voice" (1 Kings 19:12 NKJV), listening for God in silence because, as the psalmist wrote millennia ago, "to you even silence is praise" (Psalm 65:1 CEB).

Call it meditation, call it contemplative prayer, call it centering prayer, call it silent prayer—call it what you will, but it's addressing the same basic human needs: to find peace beyond all the chatter. To know who you are in the midst of endless demands on your time and the fatal allure of busyness. To observe the mind so you can give up the mind. To do more by doing less.

I love church. I've worshipped in the same place for over thirty years, singing in the choir, volunteering at the soup kitchen, teaching a class on Sunday mornings, serving on committees, sitting on boards. I don't believe my marriage would have survived and thrived without the sustenance of my faith community. I wouldn't have wanted to raise our kids without the experience of listening to Scripture, praying together, doing the annual Christmas pageant, savoring communion, singing sacred music, going on retreats, and knowing the intimacy that comes from hearing a well-crafted, well-delivered sermon to shake you out of your complacency.

But I wonder, *How often do we do serious silence in church?* Hour by hour, minute by minute, we're more likely to do just the opposite. Talk. Gab at coffee hour. Pick apart a biblical text. Pray out loud (with a few pregnant pauses). Analyze the sermon. Meet in groups to discuss an inspired text. Semiannual quiet days or prayer services attract modest crowds; they're not much competition for the daily yoga classes in our communities. We might manage to be quiet together for a little while, but then we talk about what the silence delivered. What if we just stayed with the emptiness and cultivated it? How would it speak to us then?

I once helped organize a retreat for a group of guys from church, a weekend at a monastery up the Hudson. I figured we didn't need to have too much structure. Didn't we have enough of that already? We could just go with what the brothers did, praying several times a day in the chapel with them, chanting the psalms, savoring the holy silence, going for walks outside, sitting on rocks to watch the leaves fall in the river.

It was a terrific weekend with lots of male bonding in a holy setting. But there was one criticism that was universally leveled against the retreat: we should have met as a group a couple of times. We could have done a Bible study together or tackled some interesting spiritual topic. We should have talked more. *Talk.* (And I can already see the irony of it here on the page: writing a book about silence, adding more words to the universe to argue that there should be less. Would that I were a poet, putting down just a few words packed with less-is-more power. Better yet, a minimalist artist making a sublime statement with a single stroke of the brush.)

We talk a lot about prayer at church. We're obviously supposed to do it in our spare time (*spare* time—doesn't that say a lot?). Our pastor in a recent sermon quoted a line often attributed to Martin Luther: "I have so much to do that I shall spend the first three hours in prayer." Well, what actually did Martin Luther do for those three hours? Was he on his knees the whole time? Was he reading Scripture? Was he meditating on the Lord's Prayer? Did he have his eyes open or closed? Was this his usual time of contemplative prayer? Was it like what Jesus did up on the mountain when he needed to get away from the crowd? Nobody's ever told me.

I get a weekly list of prayer requests from church, names of people who are ill or have lost a loved one or a job or are struggling with addiction and all sorts of grave problems. I am glad to be reminded of others' needs and to pray for them. It's a welcome break from self-absorption. I know some prayer warriors who make a practice of visualizing each person on that list. Someone will say, "I've kept them in prayer and meditation all week" and I'll nod my head, but what actually does that mean? Is the meditation part different from the prayer part, or do the two work hand in hand? Nobody's ever told me.

We might like the idea of mystical silence, but we're more comfortable with a PowerPoint presentation. Mysticism is the sort of thing best left to the saints, not to humble folk like us. If we want help with meditation, we'll go to a yoga studio or download an app. We'll track down that Zen teacher whose book on "sitting"—that's what she calls it—has enchanted us. Not that that's so bad; we can learn a lot from those experts. But (to repeat myself) we don't know where meditation can be found in a Christian setting or where to dig for its Christian roots. I've even heard some claim that the whole thing is un-Christian.

Many years ago, a minister and amateur historian told me that when something essential has gone missing from regular church practice, it will pop up elsewhere. In fact, it might result in the appearance of a whole new church.

He used the example of healing prayer. In the late nineteenth century, when health care became the province of well-trained doctors, many churches forgot that Jesus was a healer too. It embarrassed them, all those miracles: giving the blind sight, making the lame walk, casting out demons, halting a woman's hemorrhaging flow. Hence the appearance of the Christian Science Church and its emphasis on healing prayer. It was a corrective jolt, he said. Yes, modern medicine should be accepted for the gift it was, but no reason it couldn't work hand in glove with traditional spiritual practices. Most churches got the message, and after a while even some of the most intellectually rigorous denominations eventually incorporated healing prayer in their worship. We pray for the sick every Sunday. We might even lay on hands. We trust it makes a difference, asking for God's help, and that's good enough. (I can feel myself avoiding the phrase *faith healing* because of all sorts of mumbo jumbo associated with it.)

What about the growth of meditation in an era when churches are fading in power and popularity fast? Why is it now, when the fastest-growing faction on surveys of religious observance in America are the "nones," those affiliated with no religious group whatsoever?[2] Why are they flocking to meditation?

Is it because, in its most popular guises, you don't have to believe in God to *do* meditation? Is it that it arrives without the baggage of organized religion? Is it because it has received the blessing of Silicon Valley and enlightened business folk? Is it because you can easily fit in meditation in the middle of a busy day? You can listen to that app on your phone without being stuck in church on a beautiful Sunday or having to miss the football game on TV. Is it because it reeks of Other? Isn't a guru in exotic garb a lot more interesting looking than a guy in loafers with a button-down shirt? Which one says "spiritual"?

I don't want to trash meditation in *any* of its forms. Much of it is good and worthy. I have gained insight from teachers who don't make any pretense to faith or use any sort of Christian language. I would be a fool not to turn to their books. I have friends who go on meditation retreats and get guidance from teachers steeped in centuries of wisdom and practice. Arcane wisdom, I was going to say, but it's not arcane. It seems very practical. One friend who goes on Zen retreats tells me that a Catholic nun is often part of the group. No surprise there. The good sister is looking for more than she's getting from home. It's then that I start wondering, *Why and when did home stop delivering the goods?*

Since Jesus cares so much about our spiritual growth, why don't we still probe his teachings for that "cloud of unknowing"? Why do we utter a line from the Psalms, like "My soul waits in silence" (62:1), and then just move on to the next verse?

I don't want to halt the "nones" from heading to yoga studios. But I wish I could tell them, "You might drop by the church up the block when you're done. We do a lot of meditation ourselves. It's a rich part of our heritage going back thousands of years. We embrace it and work at it. It connects us to who we are on a deep level. It'll add to your practice, I guarantee you. Come and see. You don't have to stay for the sermon, but do the meditation with us. Bring your mat if you wish, or sit in our pews."

Or maybe I could say, "Stay for the sermon. Please stay. Because the talk will only add to the power of your silence. You might even find powerful silence in it."

I come to meditation from a Christian background. The

key difference between it and what you get on most apps is the involvement of a higher power. I have often turned to contemporary writers who understand its Christian roots and practice—Thomas Keating, Richard Rohr, Cynthia Bourgeault, and Martin Laird, to name a few. I am a real beginner compared to them. But then again, meditation is a welcome spot for amateurs. The greatest teachers of it seem to have a humility of both sharing and not pontificating. You want to join their number.

What I wish for is that the church (my church, your church, the church around the corner) offers up something that will add to what those folk are getting in the meditation room at the office or during their afternoon yoga class. Surely that's something that can happen. It might even be happening already.

What if you saw it right here on the page?

✝•✝•✝

That sign above is your cue to step into deep spiritual emptiness. You might just want to turn the page to see what comes next. But for a moment, don't see. Don't push ahead. Close your eyes. Listen to the silence.

Sweet.

One caveat about this book or anything I've ever written about prayer: As you're reading along, if you feel the urge to stop and give yourself over to a meditative moment or minutes or half hour, go for it. To stop reading might be so much better than to keep reading. These are only words. Abandon them at any moment. What you have inside of you is rich, wonderful, baffling, transformative, and fulfilling. Have at it. Which leads us to our first exercise in meditation, what I'll call a time to create space for silence. May every word I say open you up to the power of silence within you. Godspeed.

Meditative Moment
Create space for silence.

I'd like you to put down this book and take in your surroundings. Stop what you're doing and look around the room where you happen to be sitting. Gaze at the bookshelves. Notice that worn spot in the carpet. Look out the window, even if there's not much of a view. See the curtains, the window blinds, the brick wall, the leaves on the tree, the bare branches if it happens to be a cold winter day. See that passing cloud. Look up at the ceiling, the fan twirling, the light that happens to be on (or off).

When we look at things, it is usually to have some interaction with them. To take that book off the shelf, to open those blinds or close them, to consider if that cloud means there's an approaching storm, to turn the light off or on. But just for a moment, see what's there. Feel what's there. The breeze coming in from the half-open window, the rug under your toes, the sunlight on the window-sill. Don't try to change any of it or interact with it. Notice that slightly anxious thought that intruded. You noticed it, and that's enough. Now take a deep breath and sit in silence . . .

✝✝✝

Congratulations. You have just meditated. It was natural and easy. There might have even been a God part to it. That sunlight, the breeze, the good book on the shelf, the feeling of the deep breath— it's all part of God's world, and you are too. To stop and notice it is a way of giving thanks. The cell phone will buzz in your pocket soon enough; perhaps it already has. The email needs to be read and answered. But wasn't this moment precious?

As the psalmist says, "We have waited in silence on your loving-kindness, O God, in the midst of thy temple" (Psalm 48:9, Book of Common Prayer). Waiting . . . not doing, just waiting. In a temple or in the holiness of your own room.

chapter two

Pick a Time
and a Place

Find a time and find a place. A time for you to make yourself available; a place where you can sit with the divine in quiet meditation. Aim for a block of time when you know there won't be interruptions, except for the usual interruptions that will be supplied by your overthinking, overanalyzing head. *What are you doing, Rick, just sitting here doing nothing? Don't you know you've got work to do? People to call, emails to send, appointments to schedule. You should get up from here right now and do all that! Don't you know that time is money?* Pick a time that will work day after day after day. The more mundane, the better.

Funny to use that word *mundane* about something that is purported to be so exalted, so otherworldly. Shouldn't prayer take you out of the world? Well, yes, and also take you into it. It's meant to do both.

Your body knows about schedules. It gets used to those times of day when it says, *Feed me right now. I'm hungry,* and those times of night when it says, *Get me to bed. I'm exhausted.* Your body will speak up for whatever it gets used to. It asks for coffee or tea in the morning, and later, like a train running right on schedule, it requests its glass of wine or dessert after dinner (and maybe some decaf this time around). When you deck yourself out in gym clothes, it says, *Okay, I'll run,* and when you plop down in front of the computer, it grudgingly agrees, *Yes, I'll work for a while.* It prepares itself for whatever you've gotten it used to.

Why not give it some regular silence? It'll like it. It'll grow to expect it. Even if your mind doesn't seem to want to quit, this dedicated moment of silence will become part of the rhythm of your day, like going for a walk, shopping online, reading the news, checking for messages on your phone, or scanning through social media. Be brutal; be disciplined; be ruthless at protecting this quiet time. Also be kind to yourself when interruptions inevitably occur.

You're not aspiring to be a holy martyr, denying yourself pleasures for some ascetic gain. You might have read statistics somewhere that demonstrate how meditation—no matter the spiritual connection—will offer all sorts of benefits: improved concentration, better rest, more happiness, success at work. That's all fine and good, but I find if I concentrate too hard on looking for results, I lose out on some of the pleasures of the practice.

Relish doing something that is perfectly useless. For fun, for play, for joy, for love, because God *is* love. This is your little private space, your investment in yourself so that you can better invest in others. Your care for your soul will prove to be care for the world.

I once wrote a sci-fi novel about people who had a secret office hidden underground where they kept the world alive, kept wars from happening, sought to heal uncountable wounds, and made sure the globe stayed spinning, by making their prayers. They were like a spy unit monitoring the globe through a network of satellites, all for the sake of world peace and inner peace. Nobody knew what they did. Nobody had to know. They were there at crisis moments, big and little, to keep dark history from happening. I was thinking of how the prayers said in a monastery could affect the world outside without the holy band of brothers ever leaving the place, simply praying where they were.

Okay, it wasn't a fabulous novel. Not enough sex and violence, I suspect. My agent was only lukewarm on it. "Write something else," she kindly said, and I did. The novel went into a back drawer or computer folder, with a lot of other stuff to keep it company.

But there's the germ of an idea that still haunts me: the notion that the world can be saved through prayer. Though it looks like I'm giving myself quiet time and space out of the most selfish motives imaginable—because I need it desperately and would spin out of control without it—I'm doing this for the world too. Because the world is spinning out of control. Selfishness and greed and vanity threaten to destroy it any day now. The headlines are there to let me know. A quick glance through the news feed on my phone is sure to get me riled up, make me angry and afraid. Want to get people to read an article? Scare them out of their wits. I fall for it all the time.

All the more reason I need this time of inner peace, an inner quiet that is meant to be catching like a favorite song.

"Let there be peace on earth," go the words of a hymn we used to sing, "and let it begin with me."[1] Indeed. The successful purveyors of peace are ones who know it well in their souls. It starts there and spins out. They convey a spiritual centeredness that makes them the dearest of fellow travelers. When they rock the boat, asking, say, a tough question or sharing a probing thought, you don't tip over. You think, you grow. They know how to find the current and catch the waves, even enjoying the breeze when they have to tack against the wind. They are in their element.

I like to think they have a prayer closet that they go into, locking the door, turning the key, tuning out to tune in—but maybe they don't. Maybe they're always like that, the lucky souls, born that way. The bliss, the surety, the joy is always with them. Bully for them. Truth to tell, when I read the advice of some sage who makes meditation sound so easy—no distractions, always connected—I can't escape the envy. *What? You never really struggle? You never have to work at it? You never start worrying about money when you sit down to pray? Never wonder about your health instead?* I pray I never give anyone that same impression.

"To try to pray is to pray," I once wrote. "It's the only human endeavor I can think of where trying is doing."[2] I still believe that. No reason to make it any harder. Trying to do it *is* doing it. Have at it. Jump in the deep end. Don't look back. Just because it seems hard is no reason to stop. The challenge is part of the adventure.

Remember what Jesus said regarding the rich young man who wanted to reach the kingdom of God, how he should sell all his possessions and give the money to the poor? When the man went away grieving, for he had many possessions, Jesus delivered the line about how it was easier for a camel to pass through the eye of a needle than for someone rich to enter the kingdom (Matthew 19:16–26). I picture the young man walking away—no doubt thinking of all those stocks and bonds he's got squirreled away—and I want to scream, "Stick around. Listen to Jesus!" Because this is what comes next:

"With God all things are possible." Even for people like you and me.

That is the work of the day: to make the impossible possible.

Developing a practice. Indulging it. Wallowing in it. Smiling through it. Doing it day after day after day, with God. "Without him everything is nothing," said the French divine Jean-Pierre de Caussade (1675–1751) in his posthumously published *Abandonment to Divine Providence*, "and with him nothing is everything."[3] Doing nothing? Nothing doing.

I should call this book *A Prayer and Meditation Guide for People Who Really Need the Help*. Not for those who can do it as easy as breathing, who make some heavenly connection the instant they close their eyes. Not for those who take to the prayer closet like a duck to water, who might be blissfully unaware that some of the rest of us struggle at it. Not for those who sit on their mats and instantly transport to another zone.

I'm a sucker for stories about turning points, those moments when time stops. One of the most famous examples, of course, is the apostle Paul on the road to Damascus. A great persecutor of the early Jesus movement who had stood in the throng when Stephen was stoned to death, Paul (or Saul, as he was known at the time) was on that fabled road when Jesus appeared to him and asked him what he was doing. Why was he harassing the Lord?

Paul was plunged to the ground—knocked off his horse, if we see it the way the great artist Caravaggio painted it.[4] It's the gold standard for dramatic conversion, a journey interrupted and forever altered. Paul became the great champion for Jesus' message, spreading it around the Roman Empire. But the whole scene, as we envision it, comes from the book of Acts, written by Luke. Compare it to how Paul himself describes the event in his letter to the Galatians, when he simply received "a revelation of Jesus Christ" (1:12). No blindness, no road, no being thrown to the ground. Just change that begets change and more change and transforms a world.

Embracing change—not experiencing it just once but seeking it again and again and again—is at the heart of the spiritual life. I need and depend on quiet revelations that come more frequently than once in a lifetime. I need to be Paul on the road all the time. I read, I worship, I meet with friends. And I pray in silence every morning.

Give yourself a time and a place. How much time? Five minutes will do. Really. Five minutes of sitting in silence, opening up your heart, listening to your mind, putting your worries into divine hands. Five minutes twice a day—say, first thing in the morning and right before you go to bed—will work. You will relish that time. But stick to it; regularity is even more important than how much time you give. When you start saying, "I'm here," you will not be alone in sitting there. You are giving yourself a place of utter stillness and transformation. Guard it with your life.

Make it longer if you can. Nine minutes is good. Twenty minutes is golden. If it's five minutes one morning and twenty minutes the next, that's okay. Don't waste any of the precious time on self-criticism, even if that's where your mind goes. Note it and let it go.

No need to apologize to yourself. There's no rating system up there, no heavenly ranking of seraphim, cherubim, thrones and powers, with little you—little me—way down at the bottom of the spiritual hierarchy. After all, they are angels. You're merely human. But by putting yourself in that quiet place, you are putting yourself among their ranks here on earth. Take a leap at that.

I do it in the morning, first thing. Well, not exactly first thing. I go to the john first—who can pray on a full bladder?—and then shave. Then I sit.

The sofa in the TV room is one of two regular prayer places for me. There's a badly painted radiator in one corner that rattles in the winter. I can hear the traffic when a car or a truck or the garbage truck rumbles by. People are walking their dogs. Someone's car radio blasts. There's the squeak, squeak, squeak of a bicycle going up the hill. The birds can make a racket in the springtime—"Look at the birds of the air" (Matthew 6:26).

I can hear the rain blow against the windows, a plane or helicopter buzz overhead. If there's a storm brewing, the wind shakes the trees, and I might have to get up to shut a window.

I sit on a sofa with a pillow behind me. I pull my legs up under me. I admire those limber souls who can sit perfectly in a cross-legged position. I am not one of them. I don't really think how you sit is so essential—hands open or closed, legs folded under you or grounded on the floor or stretched out in front of you—as long as you're comfortable. On cold mornings I grab a blanket and swing it over my shoulders. You will consult your body—more on that to come—but you don't want to always be *thinking of* your body.

There is no TV in the TV room, but there are plenty of opportunities for distraction: the computer on my desk; the bookshelves full of dog-eared paperbacks that we couldn't possibly part company with. At any moment I could turn to them for inspiration.

Not here, not now. It's only me and silence. I close my eyes—not without checking my phone first just to see what time it is.

You can set an alarm if you wish. You can also open your

eyes to check your watch. It doesn't really matter. You will probably find that your body clocks the time very well. You'll tell yourself that you only meant to sit for twenty minutes; a thousand things will seem to happen in that time—a thousand things and nothing—and you'll think, *Gosh, I've probably gone overboard this morning. I've been in my praying place for too long. I didn't mean to meditate this long.* Then you'll open your eyes and check the time on your phone. Twenty minutes exactly.

Time expands and contracts when you put yourself in a place where time is not supposed to count.

As a friend recently reminded me, time can be measured emotionally too. The sands in the hourglass come in myriad colors, and you can feel them ping through you in different tones, like music. There are major and minor keys and jarring shots of disharmony, but then who wants to sit through a symphony that's only sweetness and light? Dissonance is part of the process. Listen to it.

You don't have to close your eyes. I have friends who stare at a point on the wall or out the window or even at a picture. As a kid I always wondered why grown-ups closed their eyes to pray. If we are told that God is everywhere, why do people shut their eyes when they want to talk to the divine? Why don't they look up to where God is, wherever *that* is?

Now I know. I'm most likely to feel and discover the God within when I sit with my eyes closed. I shut off the demanding visual stimuli—that never-ending internal TV show—so I can be aware of the vast chasm that's inside.

Others suggest that when you *do* open your eyes—when you're finished—you should sit for a minute or two to take in the experience, to transition back to the world.

Some days that works for me; some days when my time's up, I'm ready to get up right away. I stretch out my arms and release the blanket, if I'm using a blanket. One time I turned around and it looked like angel wings on the back of the sofa, ready to let me go. I'm ready to face my day. Ready to go for a run or go to the gym or eat breakfast or read the paper or log on to the computer or answer a text or an email or go to work.

Did I hear all the noises around me while I was sitting? Of course I did. Pretending that you do not hear something that you heard—the blast of the car horn, the rattling of the radiator, the plane overhead, a phone playing its song—is a perfect way to wander right out of the sacred space. *I don't want to think about that* is a sure recipe for thinking about anything. That which you pretend to bury grows into a little gremlin. That which you doggedly ignore will speak up—loudly.

Catch-and-release is a technique I've heard recommended. It makes a lot of sense: catch the distracting thought or inter-ruption, and release it. Better yet, put it into a prayer. *That song reminds me of my mom.* Pray for her. *That radiator needs to be fixed.* Pray for those who live on the streets without heat. *Can't that woman come up with a better ringtone for her phone?* becomes *Lord, help me let go of all my judgmental attitudes.* Make your prayers short. Brevity is the soul of wit. The point is, you can catch and release any of it, and all of it, to God.

It would seem that you should pick the quietest place you can find for meditation, but I would argue that it's more impor-tant to choose the most convenient place, the place that you can get to easily enough. Whatever place you pick will take on its own holy quality. You will sanctify it by your practice. Call it your prayer closet, even if it's just a lumpy sofa in a yet-to-be-decluttered room. Make it your meditation zone. You can do this to the most unlikely places. I should know. Because the other place I regularly practice meditative prayer is the New York subway.

Years ago, I wrote a book called *Finding God on the A Train*.[5] We live in Upper Manhattan, and the A train is the train I take to work. I usually get a seat where I can close out the world—although I open my eyes every now and then to see if I need to offer my seat to a pregnant woman or a guy with a cane or an elderly soul. What kind of calm do you deserve if you're not paying attention to your neighbors' needs? How will you find inner peace? As Jesus said, "You should treat people in the same way that you want people to treat you; this is the Law and the Prophets" (Matthew 7:12 CEB).

Most mornings, though, I sit on the moving train, the doors opening and closing, people getting on and off, the conductor calling out the stations, riders staring at their phones, a beggar coming through with an empty cup, friends talking to each other. (If I've plopped down next to someone really loud, I'll see if I can spot an empty seat somewhere else.) Our son Tim says he can't meditate on the train because he's afraid he'll be so zoned out that he'll miss his stop. I've never found this a problem. I like the rhythm of the stations punctuating my meditative efforts. They tell me how much time I've got. "West Fourth," the conductor says. I think, *Three more stops to get to work. Savor the moment. Listen to the silence.* The doors slam shut, the engine rumbles, and I'm off to the races.

Pick a time, pick a place. The regular place you go to pray provides all the stimulus you need. Those sounds, the smells—the coffee, the air conditioner's hum—will be triggers for your contemplation. This is your Sistine Chapel, your Lourdes, your Chartres. As more than one critic has pointed out, when Jesus told his listeners to go into their closets to pray (Matthew 6:6 KJV), he was speaking to a crowd who lived cheek by jowl—hand to mouth—and rarely had private rooms of their own for sleeping, let alone closets. Certainly not the kind of closets we're used to (though the closets in our house, if truth be told, are so stuffed with clothes and shoes and file boxes that there would be no room for a human to sit and pray).

Our TV room is a luxury, a blessing for a pair of empty nesters that doubles as the guest room whenever we have visitors. It's bigger than the proverbial closet and far more comfortable. On the other hand, the subway train on the morning commute is packed to the gills and noisy and hardly private. Yet it works just fine. With my eyes closed it's my space, better than a private jet, taking me on my journey. God seems to know when to give me a nudge so that I open my eyes and notice the pregnant woman who just stepped onto the train so I can give her my seat. I stand with my eyes closed near her, still in my zone.

Like I say, pick a time and pick a place. Insert prayer and meditation time into your routine. No need to advertise it. You don't have to tell anyone, though you can let your spouse or your kids know so he or she can save interruptions for later. If you're doing it at work, you can block out the time on your calendar and go into a huddle room as though it's a meeting (and it is). You can put on a pair of headphones and face your computer with your eyes closed. The fewer people you tell, the better. After all, Jesus urged his followers to not be like the Pharisees—to not make a big show of our sacred intentions. When I'm working on a book project, I don't tell anyone what

I'm doing. It's better to put all that creativity into the work. Same with the prayers.

Be bold. Guard the time and place jealously. Make them yours.

Meditative Moment
What's your best time and place?

One of the goals of mindfulness is to become aware of what your mind is doing. Pay attention to it. It would rather you didn't, preferring to be the cart that's driving the horse. So even without meditation or prayer, look at your schedule. Where is the slot for contemplative prayer? Where could you squeeze it in? Create a list. "I do X at 8:30 and Y at 9:15, and I like to do Z at 10:25 before I have a third cup of coffee, if there's not a meeting I have to go to . . ." Map it out.

As for the perfect place, audition it. Close your eyes and listen to what you hear. Thirty seconds is enough, maybe a minute. It's hard to concentrate exclusively on sound for too long. After you've listened, imagine this as your daily background for prayer.

How does it feel? Anything really jolt you? Mind you, we become very used to sounds over time.

We city folk go out to the country and find the rural "silence" really noisy. Those crickets, those birds, those raccoons scavenging for food in the brush—it's enough to keep you up at night. Give us the soothing rumble of traffic, air conditioners, screeching brakes, and car radios. We grow used to the noise.

Make a conscious choice about the place and stick with it. What your unconscious mind—your background meditation chatter—says about it, well, that'll be just part of your prayer life.

chapter three

Meditate on the Word

Turn to the Bible for inspiration in your meditation.

The concept of *lectio divina* is an ancient practice of taking a piece of Scripture—a parable, a verse, part of a verse, maybe just a single word—and meditating on it. There are formulaic steps for *lectio divina*, including reading the passage, praying over it (talking to God), meditating on it, going into contemplation (which can be an even deeper place to go), and finally ending with some sort of action inspired by the passage.

I like *lectio divina* because it's an enriching way to look at Scripture and a great way to focus my mind in contemplative silence. Would that I could be like the holy souls who make their way through the Bible verse by verse, reading and praying through it from beginning to end. Would that I could live that long and well. I find that turning to just one verse works as a diving board for meditation, a jumping-off point. Partly because many of the things Jesus said only make sense to me in the context of meditation, when I let them seep into my heart and mind.

Take a familiar passage, "Those who find their lives will lose them, and those who lose their lives because of me will find them," or, to use another translation, "Whoever finds their life will lose it, and whoever loses their life for my sake will find it" (Matthew 10:39 CEB, NIV). We end up stressing that "for my sake" to make it all right. We're just supposed to be less self-involved, less selfish, more interested in others for Jesus' sake, and then we're safe.

I don't think that gets us off the hook. Look at the way Luke's gospel prefaces it with, "If any man would come after me, let him deny himself, and take up his cross daily, and follow me" (9:23 ASV).

How do we deny ourselves? Our survival seems predicated on doing just the opposite. If we don't advocate for ourselves, we'll never get that job, that promotion, that raise. If we don't look out for number one, everybody is sure to walk all over us. More mundanely, if we don't make that shopping list and head off to the supermarket, there won't be anything in the refrigerator for dinner. We'll starve. Sure, we look out for our families and loved ones. But that's not denying ourselves at all; that's taking care of the network that takes care of us.

What would happen, though, if you used that verse as a motto for contemplative prayer? You close your eyes—whether you're propped up in bed or sitting on a rumbling subway—and intentionally lose yourself. You lose all the stuff you tend to cling to. The shopping lists, the to-do lists, the emails, the text messages that make themselves known. The bank balance and the worry over whether there's enough to cover the bill you need to pay or have already paid. Again and again, you let that stuff go. You don't do it just once. You do it ten times, then a hundred, then a thousand, and then so many that you've lost track because it's become routine.

Take another verse that most of us would rather skip over or mumble if we have to read it aloud: "If anyone comes to me and does not hate his own father and mother and wife and children and brothers and sisters, yes, and even his own life, he cannot be my disciple" (Luke 14:26). Okay, leave your mom and dad and family behind to make a life for yourself, but hate them?

Your wife and your children too? So much for pretty ideals of what makes the perfect Christian family. I like to imagine this as a slogan for some *Saturday Night Live* sketch on Christian parenting. Family members staring daggers at each other; "Hey, we're just doing what the Good Book says, everybody hating everybody else."

Now go back to that verse. Hold it in your head in silence for a long while. Argue with it: What in the world was Jesus thinking? Maybe he wanted to make sure the disciples left their families behind when they set out to follow him because it would be a tough road ahead. Make no bones about it: sacrifices would be called for. Discipleship had huge costs. (I always find it curious to read in the Gospels how Jesus healed Peter's mother-in-law, but we never learn what happened to Peter's wife. Who was she? Was she alive at the time? Did Peter abandon her? Was the healing of the mother-in-law some sort of consolation for Peter's departure?)

Maybe we're supposed to keep the command in its historical context. Jesus doesn't want *us* to hate our mothers and fathers and spouses and children. Nothing like it. He was simply talking to a bunch of followers two millennia ago, not us.

I don't buy that. Jesus was given to making his listeners uncomfortable. He still is. Why? Because what makes us uncomfortable has the power to change us. Take that into meditation. An uncomfortable silence isn't all bad.

Here's the way I've come to think of this verse: even in the best of families there is stuff that gets in the way of our becoming who we're meant to be—that is, who God wants us to be. When you close your eyes, a wicked family pattern might emerge. Perhaps you recover a memory of desperately wanting to please a loved one, but the special gift you gave or the picture you drew was hardly appreciated at all. Your love went unreceived.

I had parents who loved me—no doubt about it—but I continue to be surprised at how painful memories can get dredged up. Like that day I thought I was helping Mom with a cleaning project. She was outside, spraying the hose on the wall, and she needed someone to close the windows upstairs. I fumbled and pulled and couldn't do it. In exasperation she finally said, "Would you please get your brother?" Then I heard her mutter, "I've asked the wrong child."

How painful that was. Later she apologized, but still. It was there, something I held on to so tightly I couldn't possibly let it go.

Until I found myself sitting on the sofa—my body comfortable even if my soul was not—and it resurfaced. I didn't drop it back then. I'd been holding on to it—the anger, the hurt—until it took up far more room than I ever intended.

"Hate," Jesus said. That's too much. Prayer should never involve hate. But maybe hate is what I needed here, some physical expression of my anger. Like Jesus turning over the tables in his Father's house, turned into the den of thieves. Hate your own life? Hate your own loved ones? Yes, for the moment, because sometimes the family myths we cling to are not the best for us. We need to let them go.

Or to take another example, one day I was on the subway reading the Bible (Scripture on your phone or Kindle is much easier to carry around than the big Holy Book in print) when I came upon one of those dastardly passages that seem designed to make me wallow in guilt: "In the same way, none of you who are unwilling to give up all of your possessions can be my disciple" (Luke 14:33 CEB).

I closed my eyes and went into a snit fit. I wish I could say it was prayerful. *How am I supposed to give up all my possessions?* I asked. *That wouldn't be responsible. I wouldn't be able to pay for this subway ride. I wouldn't be able to fund my kids' college educations. I wouldn't have a place to live. I wouldn't have any money to retire on. I wouldn't be able to give anything to church—let alone have something for that person on the subway asking for money—if I gave up all my possessions. What am I supposed to do, Jesus?*

So much for the supposed silence I aspire to in meditation. I do yammer on in frustration. This time I added some visual imagery. I could picture the apartment, the clothes, the 401(k), the checkbook, the furniture, our bedding, my shoes, my wallet. All of my possessions. How could I give them up? Maybe I could give away some of the clothes, stuff I don't wear and don't need, but what about all the rest?

Let all those things go now, came the message. *Drop them in prayer. Give up your possessions to me. Give up their ability to possess you.*

Done. Done just once? No, done again and again. Once some clever writer did a satire of the *New York Times* lifestyle section then called "Living," which was full of articles about expensive things to own and wear and cook, not to mention the ads. In the satire it was appropriately dubbed "Having." The stuff we have, and the stuff we yearn to have, can *have* us.

I don't doubt that Jesus was talking about real things, real possessions, the junk that clutters our lives. It's even worse the way it can clutter our inner lives. Those thoughts in our heads, those concerns and worries, want to convince us that they are our survival mechanism, that if we didn't heed them, we'd go belly-up. They feel themselves threatened when we decide to embrace silence. *What? You trying to kill us? No, no, no, no.* Our silence doesn't make them softer; it increases their volume.

The reason you pay attention to them in meditation is that if you don't, they will only get more insistent, even perverse. "Forgive us our sins, as we forgive those who sin against us," Jesus taught us to pray (Luke 11:4 NLT). Forgiveness is the work of facing down the noise. It might even manifest itself in physical discomfort or pain. *Why is my back hurting me?* you might ask during meditation. *What is it about my elbow? I can feel my knee bugging me.* But what is it behind the back, the elbow, the knee? Is there some more painful memory you're blocking?

Meditation can be an adjunct to talk therapy. It's not the same and should never be considered a replacement for it. There's nothing like having a professional listen attentively, knowledgeably, therapeutically, when you're dealing with the heavy stuff of life. I've suffered from periods of depression and have been very grateful for the healing work of talk therapy. But I've also seen how contemplative prayer can be a companion to therapy. "Something came up the other day while I was sitting on the subway," I can say to my therapist. And we talk.

There is always this tension in meditation of listening to the inner noise—mindfulness—and then letting it go.

"How do you do it?" someone asked me at a writers' workshop where I had mentioned the importance of meditation.

"You sit somewhere, close your eyes, and wallow in the silence," I said, sounding holier than I wish I had.

"Every time I try to do that, all I can hear is all this distracting thought. I remember all the stuff I'm supposed to do and things I've promised to get done and dates I need to mark in my calendar and things people have said to me and things I've said to them . . . There's no way I can get calm enough to meditate."

"But that's the whole point," I said. "Sit there and listen to the noise. Just keep doing it. All that noise is what it is. It's part of meditating."

She seemed crushed. I think she wanted some sort of image of a person floating on a lotus blossom with a beatific expression on her face, a sure hallmark of prayer. The reassurance that if you just did a certain thing, took the right number of breaths, paused long enough in between them, muttered something very quiet about God's love, you could be sure to feel a meditative calm. A promise that you could wear the same beatific expression with your eyes open or closed.

"Never confuse a person's exterior with what might be going on inside," said a worthy soul. I've never taken a selfie of myself praying, and I don't intend to start. Don't really like looking at images of myself anyway. (I've had to do it often enough in professional situations, like choosing an author photo. I tend to choose the image that no one else wants, which seems to tell me that I really don't have any idea of what I truly look like. Or rather what I'd like to think I look like doesn't have much in common with the truth.)

A picture of me praying would show an expressionless face.

A picture of me praying would say *nothing* about what's really going on inside.

Just to be certain, I checked a journal entry from a couple of years ago. Here's what it said:

There is a lot of planning going on in my head when I'm supposed to be meditating—when I am meditating. Thinking about what we're supposed to do this weekend, how will it all fit in? There's the Men's Clean-Up Day at church. (How many guys are going to come? Will we have enough people? Is it BYOB for the after-party?) I've got to visit X, who is recovering from surgery. He was so good to visit me in the hospital. Would Y be able to come with me? That would be fun . . . which night will I be home this week for dinner? Thursday? Where shall I take C for our anniversary dinner? Better make a reservation. And get some chocolates . . . don't have any wrapping paper for them.

I can imagine someone reading that and saying, "Okay, that's just the part you do *before* you pray. You go through all that and then clear your head."

I've come to believe that all that noise *is* the prayer. Paying attention to the noise, being in a place where I have to hear it, not thinking better of myself or feeling holier-than-thou. Being Rick, who has tons of distracting thoughts when he prays.

Here's the most important thing I can say about such distractions: *don't shut them out, and don't do anything about them.* Not while you're praying. Not while you're sitting there. Don't get up and scribble notes to yourself. Don't open your eyes and log on to your computer before you go back to prayer. Don't do anything practical about that stuff that's there. It will still be there when you open your eyes two minutes later or thirty minutes later. If it's important, it won't go away. It's testing you—yes, these are the "temptations" we don't want to be led into. The noise wants to tell you that it is more important than anything else that's going to happen while you're meditating. *Me! Me! Me!* it cries. *Listen to me!*

As if not doing so would mean losing your life.

As in losing your life to find it.

Noticing what's going on is a necessary step to forgetting it.

"Forget what you know," wrote the anonymous author of *The Cloud of Unknowing.* "Forget everything God made and everybody who exists and everything that's going on in the world, until your thought and emotions aren't focused on or reaching toward anything, not in a general way and not in any particular way. Let them be."[1]

This is the work of contemplative prayer. If it sounds hard, that's a good thing. That's the pleasure, the challenge. Jesus commanded his followers, "Go in through the narrow gate. The gate that leads to destruction is broad and the road wide, so many people enter through it. But the gate that leads to life is narrow and the road difficult, so few people find it" (Matthew 7:13–20 CEB).

Narrow, difficult. There is a paradox here. We are welcoming, affirming when we express our faith. We want everyone to know that God loves them, that God shows no partiality. But there is also this more challenging aspect of faith: "Go in through the narrow gate." It's not just about taking the ethical high road, living a pure, blameless life while resisting the temptations of self-righteousness that can be found along that way. Fine and good. Then put yourself on the difficult up-and-down, back-and-forth road of meditation. Look at all those roadblocks that make for rough traveling. Get rid of them. Cut them out; rip them up.

"And if your right eye causes you to fall into sin, tear it out and throw it away," Jesus said in another one of those passages that seem ripe for parody. "It's better that you lose a part of your body than that your whole body be thrown into hell. And if your right hand causes you to fall into sin, chop it off and throw it away. It's better that you lose a part of your body than that your whole body go into hell" (Matthew 5:29–30 CEB).

Is he asking us to mutilate ourselves, to grab a knife or sharp pair of scissors and cut off various offending parts? Goodness, if I started doing that there would be very little of me left, and what remained would be covered in scars. A bloody mess.

Words like "sin" and "hell" seem out of place here for what is a so-called peaceful practice. But meditation can be a chance for spiritual vivisection. The cutting out of the right eye, the tearing off of the right hand. All sorts of demons might make themselves known in the process. Envy, pride, petty jealousies, lust, greed, fantasies of power. Hear them out. Acknowledge their existence. Then do the cutting out and the tearing off. Again and again.

Does this sound like hard work? Better than living with those things.

The author of *The Cloud of Unknowing* suggested concentrating on a single word during contemplation, preferably a one-syllable word. Unsurprisingly, the writer suggested *God*. I like doing that. I find that I can even chant it on a single note—when you chant on a moving subway train, no one else can hear you. It is a note that plays quietly within me, deeply resonating. But the author also suggested the word *sin*, something I'm far less likely to take on, for obvious, squeamish reasons. Who likes sin? Why invite contemplation of that? Doesn't it sound like the manipulative harangue of a two-bit preacher on the sawdust trail, offering salvation to wounded souls for just the right price? Get saved or go to hell. Concentrate on your sin. Sin, sin, sin.

Contrary to what you might think, in meditation that can be altogether purifying. Because to note sin is to let it go, to get the monkey off your back, to observe the fears so they don't control you. To ask for forgiveness and go on, really go on. As the old saying goes, courage is fear that has said its prayers.[2]

I like the image from the *Cloud of Unknowing*:

> If your word is *sin,* focus on sin as a lump, impenetrable to your mind, but none other than yourself. I believe when you're engaged in this dark, simple awareness of sin as a hard lump (synonymous with you), there could be no more insane creature than you are then—you'll doubt your ability to live outside a strait jacket. But you won't look insane. No one will even guess you feel this way because your exterior will remain calm, and anyone looking at you will think all is well, since none of this inner turmoil is reflected in your face or body language. Sitting, walking, lying down, leaning, standing, or kneeling, you'll appear fully at ease, unruffled and restful.[3]

Try *sin* as a word to focus on. See what it brings you or where it takes you. And of course, try *God*. No matter what you're doing, the goal is connection to God. The motivation is love of God and for God. The practice is bringing your life before God and listening to where God will take you.

Look for biblical words, especially one-syllable words, that you can use to focus on in meditative prayer: like I've mentioned, *God, sin, Christ, Lord, strength, rest, soul, wait, heart, bless, faith, hope, love, psalm, praise, light, word, joy.* Or take some longer words, like *fortress, refuge, righteous, holiness, presence, heaven, blessing, everlasting, goodness, compassion,* and of course, *Jesus Christ.* Such words are rich with meaning. To concentrate on just one is to open yourself up to an inner world and to circle away from your aimless wanderings.

I don't know exactly what Martin Luther did for those three hours that he devoted to prayer. I don't know what a lot of devout folk do in their quiet meditative time. But see if any of this will help you. It's the narrow gate I leap through every day.

Meditative Moment

Pray one word.

So many biblical words have dropped from everyday use. Take a simple concept like mercy. "Have mercy on me," we pray. We ask for God's mercy. We mercifully request favor. In times past when an all-powerful king could alter a person's life with a wave of the royal hand, asking for mercy would have had more significance. You could say to a person, "Have mercy on me." Our power structures are a little more subtle today—I've never said to my boss, "Have mercy on me" when I've messed up, although I've thought it.

All the more reason to restore the power of such words in prayer. I have often turned to the ancient Jesus Prayer, "Lord Jesus Christ, have mercy on me." It reminds me of the need for God in my life. It restores a right relationship.

Got your word? Go for it right now.

†·†·†

To pick a word and meditate on it is to let go of the tyranny of the mind. God gave us multiple faculties, which is exactly what the Bible shows us. The crowds hung on to Jesus' every word, but often his presence was more than enough. The woman who was healed of an enduring hemorrhage that baffled all physicians could be transformed by simply touching the hem of his robe.

A word, a very powerful word, can take you to a place that's beyond words. One word—one you can use over and over again—can be enough. Make it your tool.

chapter four

Listen to Your Anger

When you meditate, look to the things that irritate you.
The big things aren't the best measure of a spiritual life, at least not for me. The little things, the day-to-day irritations, are what keep me sitting on that sofa, what keep me returning to my practice, what have me digging deeper in meditation. Yes, the prospect of death always looms, and fears about my physical health can send me down a rabbit hole of anxiety—all that deserves another chapter—but there's something I think of as the Irritation Index that lets me know how I'm doing when it comes to loving God and loving my neighbor as myself.

"Whenever anything disagreeable or displeasing happens to you, remember Christ crucified and be silent," said John of the Cross, another one of those mystics I turn to for help in my prayer life.[1] Thomas Keating emphasized, "Silence is God's first language."[2]

So what does the silence say to me? I'm reminded of my own failings.

The biggest challenge for me is my own self-confidence, cloaking a secret or not-so-secret self-righteousness. I'm basically a mild-mannered fellow, right? No deep anger. Nothing terribly complicated going on. Call me Mister Rogers. Mister Nice Guy. What you see is what you get. Got that, God?

But get me behind the wheel of a car and there is the Big Reveal. Farewell, Mister Nice Guy. "The only time you ever swear is when you're driving," a friend pointed out. How true.

I shock even myself. Where did I get that tongue? That's not really me. Or is it?

There I am on the highway, in the fast lane, a truck tailgating me. *I'm sure his days are tougher than mine*, I say to myself. *He's probably been driving for the last sixteen hours.* Graciously, ever so graciously, I move to the right lane, letting him pass. He plows on ahead. No honk of thanks, no wave, no friendly smile, but why should that bother me? I feel good about myself. I'm such a mensch. I poke along in the slower lane for a couple of minutes, full of self-congratulatory goodwill. I tell myself that prayer has opened me up to being more generous, more understanding, helping me become a good person.

I'm ready to move back into the fast lane because, truth to tell, I hate going sixty miles per hour when I could go seventy, and I hate having people passing me. I signal politely. I'm going to move into the fast lane again.

But what do you know? The lady ahead of me darts in, taking my place (why should I think of it as *my* place?), taking no notice of me. She zips off at seventy miles per hour, without a moment's nod in my direction. It makes me furious. I blurt a few choice words. Why should it matter? No one else can hear them. Just me. (And God.)

Finally, I cool off a little. And yes, I get to move into the fast lane. I've lost two or three minutes at most, nothing substantial. It's not like I'm running late to an important meeting. And gosh, at seventy miles per hour, I could easily make up the lost time. I'm moving ahead. It's all fine. But part of me thinks I'm not going anywhere, that I'm stuck in neutral. I'm still peeved at that lady who pulled in front of me. This is just what a prayer life is for.

File it away. Put it in the Irritation Index. You thought this holy time on the cushion or bench was all about thinking lovely, sublime thoughts? Sure, some of the time. It's also about paying attention to all those irritants, the stuff that gets stuck in your craw, the incidents you wish you didn't have to pay any attention to, the ones that you could forget but that come careening back into your meditative time, demanding your focus. There's a reason they irritate you. That very irritation is worth paying heed to.

During my meditation time the next morning, when I found myself remembering that incident on the highway, I had to circle back to the angry side of Rick. Hear it, notice it. Ask God to forgive me for not loving my neighbor. That was the time to begin to change.

The word *sin* is probably most readily connected to sexual sins in many people's minds. Remember that old expression "living in sin"? There's something alluring about it, with a wink-wink and nudge-nudge. *Lucky for them to be living in sin.* But the bigger, more dangerous sins, as far as I'm concerned, are ones of pride, arrogance, self-promotion, self-righteousness, self-involvement, greed, petty-mindedness, narcissism, and paying homage to the world's false gods.

People can irritate me. In fact, they can drive me nuts. Their neediness, their fretting, their self-absorption, their insecurity, their tireless braggadocio. But if I look closely, it's often the very similarity of their faults to my own—that nagging familiarity—that is the fingernail scratching on the inner blackboard. I'm projecting my faults onto them.

In job interviews, after candidates have enumerated their many strengths, they're often asked, "What would you say your weaknesses are?" One of the most popular responses is to say, "Impatience. I like to get things done." Or "I'm a perfectionist. I want everything to be just right." How quick we are to pick a weakness that makes us look strong. *Golly, I'd better hire that woman who says she's impatient. She might get on some people's nerves but at least she'll get the job done.* Or *We sure could use a perfectionist around here.*

How hard it is to admit to deeper, more unpleasant truths. Maybe not in a job interview, but why not when we're alone? Why not sit with the raw truths in silence instead of running away from them, creating unholy emptiness with empty busyness? Silence *is* God's language.

"Prayer doesn't change God; prayer changes us," goes the old saying. In our heart of hearts, what we all want is transformation. That means admitting what is wrong. Even harder, it means uncovering the wrongs, ferreting them out.

I was once volunteering at our church soup kitchen. I usually work the floor, greeting our guests, resetting the tables when people leave, making announcements, bursting out in song—recalling my college days when I worked one summer as a singing waiter.

You get to know the guests all too well, and there is this one lady who always has to sit in a corner, spreading out so that no one can sit near her. She takes forever eating, not allowing us to reset her place so others can be served.

On this day we were really stressed. We had too many guests and not enough volunteers. I kept telling myself that at least I was quick at turning the tables, wiping them up and resetting them. If only we had a little more help. Just then the lady in the corner spilled her coffee. I dashed forward with the sponge and a stiff smile. "No problem. Glad to help. Oh, you'd like another cup of coffee? Sure. Let me get it." (Watch and see how fast and efficient I can be, even under pressure. What a champ.)

I got that second cup of coffee, remembering that she likes extra cream and extra sugar (though I was thinking that she shouldn't have all that sugar—she was prediabetic, no doubt). I brought the cup and put it down in front of her. No sooner had I dashed heroically across the room to reset three other places than she spilled the coffee again.

This time I wasn't particularly gracious about it. "We're really short-staffed today," I said. "I can't believe you spilled your coffee twice. What's wrong with you?"

What a jerk I was. This wasn't really saintly behavior.

In a minute I managed to blurt out apologetically, "I'm sure your life is more difficult than mine." But my buttons had been pushed and I'd responded.

The thing that popped up later in the quiet—or noise—of my meditative practice was the similarity of the soup kitchen incident to my irritation behind the wheel of the car. It hadn't been the thing done to me that bothered me. It was the attack on my self-image, the deflating of the kind, generous, bighearted person I like to think I am. I'm not really Mister Rogers at all.

I think again of the rich man who asked Jesus what he had to do to obtain eternal life. "You know the commandments," Jesus told him. "'You shall not commit adultery, you shall not murder, you shall not steal, you shall not give false testimony, honor your father and mother.'"

You can sense the smug self-satisfaction in the rich young man's answer: "All these I have kept since I was a boy," he said. The Eagle Scout of biblical perfection.

"You still lack one thing," Jesus said, ready to take him down a notch—or up. "Sell everything you have and give to the poor, and you will have treasure in heaven. Then come, follow me" (Luke 18:20–22 NIV).

When the man heard these words, he walked away in sadness because he was extremely rich. He couldn't walk away from his wealth. It was too much to ask. Even more, I think it was his pride that sent him packing. He couldn't wait to tell Jesus what a good man he was, how observant, how perfect at keeping the commandments. Jesus returned the favor by letting him stare at his own inadequacies, truly confront them. It was more than he could bear.

As I said earlier, a part of me yearns for the young man to stick around. To call out to Jesus, "Hey, let's talk about this. Let's figure out a way. I *do* want to follow you. But as you can see, I need help. I'm not exactly the person I say I am. You've pointed that out. Let me change. Give me a hand."

In the rich man's absence, Jesus went on to say, famously, that it is easier for a camel to go through the eye of a needle than a rich man to enter the kingdom of heaven—scaring the bejesus out of most of us—but then Jesus granted that nothing is impossible for God. I don't see that as just a bone being tossed to the privileged or an early Christian copyist's addition to a text that wasn't going to earn him enough money for parchment. Finding our way to the impossible *is* what we do when we pray. Nothing *is* impossible for God. Not if we allow ourselves to be fully human.

"Seek in reading and you will find in meditation; knock in prayer and it will be opened to you in contemplation," said John of the Cross.[3]

The Irritation Index is not something I write down. I don't keep an Excel spreadsheet. But as I sit in silence, I become more aware than ever of my failings. If you don't know who you are, how can God ever help you to become who you want to be? It's not always about fixing the stuff that's wrong. It's about hearing it. Listening.

I think of the Irritation Index as a measure for how I'm doing spiritually, my reality check. The people we love most can be just the ones we drive crazy the most and who drive us crazy. "It's 'I do' and 'You don't' and 'Nobody said that' and 'Who brought the subject up first?'" go the lyrics of an old Stephen Sondheim song about marriage from the musical *Company*, sung on the original Broadway album by the astringent Elaine Stritch and cast (boy, am I ever dating myself by this reference).[4] Love doesn't always express itself in lovely phrases.

"Honey, I love you . . . but why do you never hang up your towel?" "Why am I always the one who has to refill the toilet paper roll?" "Why did you leave that light on in the kitchen if nobody's in there?" "Well, why didn't you turn it off?" "Did you hear yourself snore last night?" "How could I? I was asleep. Just tap me on the shoulder when it bothers you." "I did. Three times." "I asked you to get low-fat milk, not nonfat, at the supermarket. Didn't you see it on my list?" "You never told me so-and-so was coming for dinner on Thursday." "Don't you ever read my emails?"

I remember a moment on our honeymoon. My wife and I were having dinner at a favorite trattoria in Florence, Italy, and I was going off on some tangent about art or architecture or music or whatever, full of profound insights. She stared at me with loving eyes—or so I thought—and I could imagine that she was thinking something like, *I'm so lucky I married Rick.* Finally, after I had gone on for too long, pasta sauce no doubt dribbling down my chin, she declared, "Don't you ever use a napkin?"

Don't you ever use a napkin? The real thought bubble over her head should have said, *What am I going to do for the rest of my life with a husband who never wipes his face?*

Honesty is essential to love; honesty in everything. I was not hurt by what my wife said—taken down a notch or two, yes—and I continue to be grateful for her oversight, pointing out stuff in me before I make an utter fool of myself, saving me from myself. I love marriage and find it a crucible for self-deception, a clearinghouse for foolish pride. I have sometimes joked with friends, saying, "How could you know anything about forgiveness until you get married?" How could you know how much you need to be forgiven?

I don't like hurting the ones I love. I want to be aware of what bothers them because it helps me know myself better, even if it's painful. Similarly, I need to pay attention to what sets me off, what irritates me. Once again, the myth of meditative prayer is that it takes us to some sublime, out-of-the-world places. Yes, that's possible. It can also take us right back to ourselves. Right back to the internal voices that cry out, *It's not fair!* In our silence we replay scenes from the recent and distant past. God means for us to listen and watch very closely.

The best of Jesus' parables catch you where you are. Don't we all sometimes feel like the good brother of the Prodigal Son, the one who stuck around at home and didn't squander his inheritance? Why should the wastrel son get the fatted calf and the big celebratory dinner? Why shouldn't it go to the dutiful, hardworking, ever-patient son who never did anything wrong, who never complained? Why shouldn't it go to us? To me? It doesn't seem fair.

Or take another example, the story of the landowner who hired day laborers for his vineyard. (I can see the whole thing happening in the wine country of Northern California, the proprietor getting the biggest bang for his buck.) He hired some workers first thing in the morning, promising them a good day's wage. They headed out into the fields.

Then he hired more workers later that morning, promising them the same. And more around noon—there must have been many vines. He even hired laborers in the late afternoon as the sun was sinking in the sky.

It was only at the end of the day that trouble hit. The manager started doling out the money, and everybody got the same amount, a day's wages. The ones who'd worked all day, from dawn to dusk, got exactly as much as those who'd worked for just the last few hours. No differences were accounted for; nobody was singled out. Of course, the ones who'd worked all day complained. It just wasn't fair! They deserved more, didn't they?

The landowner was unapologetic. Hadn't he given them what he had promised? Wasn't that the deal? "Don't I have the right to do what I want with what belongs to me?" he asked (Matthew 20:15 CEB). "Or are you resentful because I'm generous?" (Narrow-minded selfishness can so easily get in the way of our acknowledging anyone's generosity.)

Then Jesus issued the clincher: "Those who are last will be first. And those who are first will be last" (v. 16). That's us. We're both the one complaining, "That's not fair," and the one who signed up at the very last minute to labor in the vineyards.

How many times in a workplace setting have you thought to yourself, *That's not fair*? Don't you need to put that thought in a prayer?

I think Jesus wants us to confront our least-generous instincts and thoughts. It's not something we do in a crowd or by committee. We can't brag or show off when there's only an audience of one. No chance for painful honesty there. We need to go off by ourselves, the first to be last. Sometimes it's a mystery to me that Jesus would go off by himself so frequently, as the Bible says, to pray. Why? Doesn't he, of all people, have a direct line to God? Why should he have to make such effort to be alone?

I think it's because, in an example of his shared humanity, he needed to hear *himself*, remember himself, recover himself in silence, just like we do. When we're alone like that, we are in a divine one-on-one, wholly, significantly un-alone.

Meditative Moment
Notice your irritation. Listen to your angry self.

We want to be nice. We want to be kind and thoughtful. And yet sometimes it's at those moments that irritability speaks up. You're trying to do a good deed, say, and all at once it's not patience that comes out of your mouth but orneriness. People don't seem to realize how generous and kind you are!

Don't fight the negative emotions. Go with

them. That doesn't mean you have to burst out in anger at some recovered memory, but hear the rage inside. You thought sitting in silence would mean lots of peace and quiet? Instead, your emotions are pulling you in a different direction.

You are not your emotions, and that's what you're here to find out. When you fight the tiger, it becomes a monster. When you look at it with curiosity, it shrinks to the size of a kitty cat.

Close your eyes. Listen to that side of yourself you'd rather not hear. God can't help you with it till you acknowledge it. If need be, write your feelings down. Anger, jealousy, fear, self-hatred, despair. "It makes me so mad when you . . ." Fill in the blank. Then let those feelings go—in silence.

✝·✝·✝

We like to think that spiritual communities are peopled by paragons of virtue. But we all bring who we are when we come to God's table. "Community is that place where the person you least want to live with always lives," said Parker Palmer.[5]

"Love your enemies," Jesus said (Matthew 5:44). That would include those parts of ourselves we try to avoid.

chapter five

Hear the Worries

B e aware. Be intensely aware of what's going on around you and inside of you. If you're like me, you'll discover that you're worried.

We tend to be proud of our worries. We cling to them and let them identify us. Not for nothing—don't they make us who we are? Don't they keep us out of harm's way, and can't we give them credit for our good work? After all, it is my worrying self who forced me to go back over this manuscript, making sure everything made sense—*Goodness, I fear I haven't made myself clear*—checking to see that I haven't left out a word, dotting the i's and crossing the t's (spell-check might be nice, but sometimes it corrects things incorrectly).

And yet when we cling too tightly to worry, wrap ourselves inside it, it can choke us. I remember an analogy made many years ago by the psychologist and writer Eda LeShan (married to Lawrence LeShan, who authored one of the first and most popular how-to books about meditation back in the 1970s[1]). She said that our worries, if kept behind us, could be like a little motor in the back of our heads, motivating us to move forward, driving us on our way. On the other hand, if we put them in front, they could strangle us. I pictured a scarf wrapped around my neck, caught in a flywheel, choking me to death. It's not the worry itself; it's what we do with it that matters.

Those worries can get me out of bed in the morning to go after all the stuff I need to get done. That email I have to send, the meeting I should prepare for, that article I must read, the memo I should write, the bill that must get paid. Spiritually, too, worries can motivate me. There's the church committee I want to volunteer for, the passage I need to reread, the loved one I was going to pray for. And if I don't go to the soup kitchen today, will there be enough people there? But there comes a time I have to let it all go.

Jesus had a lot to say about worry: "Therefore I tell you, do not worry about your life, what you will eat or drink; or about your body, what you will wear. Is not life more than food, and the body more than clothes?" (Matthew 6:25 NIV). In principle, there's truth to that. I can work my fingers to the bone to feed and clothe and house myself and my family, but if I only did that, I would have no life, and neither would they.

"Look at the birds of the air," Jesus went on to say; "They do not sow or reap or store away in barns, and yet your heavenly Father feeds them. Are you not much more valuable than they? Can any one of you by worrying add a single hour to your life?" (vv. 26–27 NIV). Yes, yes, so true.

Then I pause for a moment and scratch my head. Geez, if I didn't worry at all, I probably wouldn't do some of those things that are important for my health, like take the daily dose of baby aspirin or the vitamin B_{12} tablets or those pills the doctor prescribed for my blood pressure. I probably wouldn't go to the gym or jog around the park. Maybe a little worry prevents me from indulging in fudge brownies or big dishes of ice cream two or three times a day instead of being satisfied with an apple or a bowl of fruit.

I can imagine Jesus smiling, seeing if I've really caught his drift. Those birds of the air, for instance. Do they really forgo all work? On my morning runs I delight in watching raptors swirl-ing overhead, constantly on the lookout, ready to plunge from the air in a minute and catch their prey. I pass the humming-birds in the bushes, tireless in gathering nectar, or the robins in spring, building their nests. Maybe they don't have barns to store their food or farms where they till it, but they're constantly on the job.

"Consider the lilies of the field," Jesus said, "how they grow; they toil not, neither do they spin: yet I say unto you, that even Solomon in all his glory was not arrayed like one of these" (vv. 28–29 ASV). When I consider the lilies of the field—oh, what joy—it looks to me like they're constantly toiling, in secret perhaps. They draw nutrients and water from the soil, using sunlight to power their photosynthesis factories. Yes, they're gloriously clothed, but it's hardly without effort. No worries, per-haps, but plenty of work. They burst on the springtime scene, giving us a glimpse of heavenly beauty, and then they're gone, which seems to be the larger point.

"But if God so clothes the grass of the field," Jesus said, "which today is alive and tomorrow is thrown into the oven, will he not much more clothe you, O you of little faith?" (v. 30). It's the work that counts, not the worries. Death is right around the corner, that fleeting glory giving added luster to the flowers, so listen to nature; pay attention; watch it; observe; consider the birds and lilies and let them guide you in your meditation and prayers.

Listening to the silence means hearing the noise.

The birds of the air make an unholy racket outside our windows as springtime approaches. Even before dawn I can hear them flutter and caw and dive and dart and call to each other as they gather their food and build their nests and prepare for the day and greet the warming air. Some of them have clocked unimaginable mileage following the seasons; others have huddled in dark corners and hidden behind bushes, happy for handouts—a few crumbs—as they've weathered the winter.

"Shut up," I want to tell them, "and let me sleep a little more." But they're insistent as Jesus is, and I finally do get up, and after going to the john and washing my face and shaving, I sit on the sofa and close my eyes and hear them.

Look at the birds of the air. Consider the lilies. These oft-quoted lines of Jesus are perfect guides to meditative prayer. Yes, we listen to the silence, finding that quiet place inside that is God working within us. But then we also listen to the noise around us, both letting it go and looking for what it's saying.

> Therefore do not worry, saying, "What will we eat?" or "What will we drink?" or "What will we wear?" For it is the Gentiles who strive for all these things; and indeed your heavenly Father knows that you need all these things. But strive first for the kingdom of God and his righteousness, and all these things will be given to you as well. (vv. 31–33 NRSV)

Keep first things first. Use your word—*God, God, God*, or *Sin, sin, sin*, if that's your choice—to keep you focused on what is important, but hear the noise. Hear what's happening around you. Pay attention.

The other day my wife and I were coming home from a class we were taking at church. She brought up something that upset her—it didn't really have anything to do with the class. She was at her wit's end. She didn't know how to handle the problem.

At first, I did the typical type-A boss thing, putting on my problem-solving persona, ready to tell her how to fix the situation and how to make it right. Who to call, what to say, how to rethink it. This is something many husbands do, and it's not always good. She saw it coming miles away and shot me a warning glance, maybe said a quick word. Only because we've talked about it before did I get her drift: *Shut up. Don't talk. Don't be Mister Fix-It. Don't be the hero you think you should be. Just listen.*

I listened carefully. It was hard. And that's what made it so valuable. I felt terrible for her. I sensed her misery. I heard her words. I felt her pain.

Later she said to me, "That was so helpful. That was exactly what I needed."

The situation actually got solved in ways neither of us could have expected. But that wasn't really the issue. Loving someone means listening to that person. This is exactly what prayer is about. Loving is listening on a cosmic scale and in the smallest, most intimate ways.

Let me circle back to worry here. The instinct with a worry is to fix it, like I wanted to with my wife. To get rid of the worry. Solve the problem. Done and over with. But notice how much better it is to simply stop and listen, calling on much greater resources than your own.

When I hear people exclaim that they do their best praying when they're doing something else, like the pastor who told me that he prays while jogging every morning or the woman who says she uses her morning commute in her car for meditation, I nod in agreement—and then wonder. Spiritual multitasking is good for keeping focus on God throughout the day. But contemplative prayer demands our full attention. Walking and meditating seems possible to me . . . but running? I know that when I'm jogging in the park, I'll utter a prayer on occasion and gaze at the view with awe, but then I'll think as I huff and puff up a hill, *Did this hill grow higher over the weekend? What is that pain in my knee? Does my form look as bad as I think it does?*

The worries quickly crowd in without any room for dispersion.

If I'm driving—we've already talked about this—I'm thinking about the creep who just butted in front of me or the traffic that's holding me back or the cop ahead who made me realize I'm well over the speed limit. Maybe I'm not as holy as the minister who finds his runs the best time for prayer or that nice woman who meditates in her car. I know what they're talking about. Listening to a Bible podcast or a psalm on a run isn't the same as sitting and closing out all distractions. ("Sitting"—that's what one of my meditating friends calls it, a term I like. Sitting in the Presence.)

I need the dedicated time alone to concentrate. I don't trust myself and the possibilities of spiritual growth without it. I don't want to be focused on anything else but what I'm doing. Otherwise, the worries will drive the bus. There has to be a reason Jesus went off by himself to pray, why it is said that the profound archbishop Desmond Tutu gets up at an ungodly early hour to pray before he does anything else, why Martin Luther spent three hours in prayer. Those people who transformed the world knew that the first step was to transform themselves, to think about the burdens they carried and how to let them go. Prayer and meditation need to be given top priority, not just conveniently fitted in.

To pray is to be aware, intensely aware, of what is going on around you. To pay attention and then to go back to what you are doing.

As I've said, I use subway time as prayer time. (Is this just like driving a car for other commuters? It doesn't feel like it. After all, I can shut my eyes. I don't have to focus on a road or stop signs or signals.) Not just while I'm going to work; I pray on my way to church or to the soup kitchen or heading home from a doctor's visit. I close my eyes and lose myself, opening them sometimes at a station to figure out where we are.

One evening I opened them about halfway through the commute, at 59th Street. From there the A train runs express, uninterrupted through to 125th Street, something I treasure. No station stops, no people getting on or off, no announcements from the conductor (usually), just the rumble of the train and the spinning of the wheels.

That evening, though, a neighbor got on, checked to see where the empty seats were, and sat right next to me. She too was coming home from a long day at work. She was listening to music or a book on tape through her earbuds. She didn't notice me at first. *Close your eyes, Rick*, I thought. *Pretend you don't see her.* But that seemed pretty phony. "Hi, Margaret," I said.

"Hi," she said with a smile of recognition. She took her earbuds out, ready to do the polite thing: to chat about our kids or our work or the neighborhood. But I could see from her face that she'd really rather be listening to whatever was coming through those earbuds. And I was ready to continue my silence.

"What are you listening to?" I asked.

"This really interesting book . . ."

"Why don't you keep listening to it? We can talk starting at 145th."

"It's a deal," she said, and she put her earbuds back in.

We both went back into our separate worlds, hundreds of miles away. At 145th Street, we came back into each other's universes, chatting amiably till we got off the train at the 181st Street station, took the elevator up, and walked through the park to our respective homes.

The people you know best, the people who understand you, will respect your silence. They need theirs too. Don't be shy about asserting yourself and your needs. No one has to know what you're doing with your eyes closed or what you're thinking. I find that when I do come up for air, the time with others is even more precious, better used, more treasured.

I ran into Margaret a couple of days later. She had told her husband about our encounter on the subway. "He thought it a perfect sign of friendship." Being silent with someone is. Same as being silent with God.

The poet John Greenleaf Whittier was a Quaker and therefore understood through habitual practice the power to be found in silence. After all, at a gathering of Friends there is no sermon, no preacher, no formal liturgy—just the urging of the Spirit. In one of his poems, the lyrics to a favorite hymn, he writes:

> O Sabbath rest by Galilee!
> O calm of hills above,
> Where Jesus knelt to share with thee
> The silence of eternity,
> Interpreted by love!

It's love that lets us understand the silence—love, the great translator.

Drop thy still dews of quietness,

Till all our strivings cease;

Take from our souls the strain and stress,

And let our ordered lives confess

The beauty of thy peace.

Here we're able to find that peace we yearn for in all our being.

Breathe through the heats of our desire

Thy coolness and thy balm;

Let sense be dumb, let flesh retire;

Speak through the earthquake, wind, and fire,

O still, small voice of calm.[2]

Meditative Moment

Use your senses, all five of them.

In your usual meditative spot, close your eyes and listen. Just listen. Do it for only thirty seconds, a minute at most. Notice what your ears hear. A symphony? Cacophony? Distinguish each sound. Where does that hum come from? What is that rumble? You'll be amazed, as I always am, how rich our world is in sound. For survival we tend to close out much of it or focus on just one sound or another. But for these next thirty seconds, hear it all.

┆·┆·┆

Now with your eyes opened, look around you for thirty seconds. See what's in the foreground, the background, maybe what's out a window, what's in your lap. Notice the colors. See the light. The grain of wood on a desk, the fading cover of a book, the water in a cup.

┆·┆·┆

Now feel the ground beneath your toes or the carpet or the cushion. Feel the fabric in your hands. Feel the pain or the freedom from pain in your various muscles. Work your way up slowly from your feet to the top of your head. Run your hands through your hair or across your face. Use the tips of your fingers to tap your knees or chest or forehead.

Don't do it for long. You can't isolate different senses for very long. Like I say, thirty seconds is a lot.

┆·┆·┆

Smell now. Smells are noted memory joggers. One faint whiff of a gardenia and I'm at my high school prom. The smell of a cigarette and I'm reminded of a beloved—and heavy-smoking—aunt. The clean scent of asphalt after a rain and I'm in the driveway of my childhood home. Stop and smell the roses? Smelling itself can make us stop.

And the next time you sit down for a meal, savor what you're eating. Stop reading, stop talking so you can just taste—and smell—the goodness of the world. "O taste and see that the LORD is good" (Psalm 34:8 KJV). After all, the Lord showed himself in the context of a meal. "Take, eat: this is my body," he said (Mark 14:22 KJV).

Taking little moments of focusing on one sense at a time is something you can do all day long to practice quiet moments of gratitude and prayer.

chapter six

Just Try Praying . . . and You'll Be Doing It!

Intention is everything. Trying is more than enough. To try to pray *is* to pray. It's the same with meditation, or with anything that involves giving up and trusting.

This seems so wrong to us though. We're results oriented. We want to do something and then quantify the difference it has made. Even in meditation we point to studies that show its benefits. People sleep better, think better, focus better, do better at the office, and lead happier, healthier, more fulfilled lives after a sustained practice. You might have heard about the Tibetan Buddhist monk who'd logged thousands of hours of meditation.[1] He was brought to the States and given multiple tests, including a scan that proved he was the happiest person on earth—or at least they called him that. His brain cells showed it. All that sitting and thinking about nothing was worth it. It paid off. We should all be so lucky.

Tangible results—that's what we want. Didn't Jesus promise that our prayers would always be answered? That old cliché that God's answers could be "Yes," "No," or "Wait" just doesn't cut it. We want to hear how the prayer for X produced X, not Y or Z. The woman prays for the perfect life partner, a six-foot-one businessman, good-looking but not too good-looking, kind, thoughtful, good-humored, a person of faith. And who should she happen to meet through the match-up site? The very man—down to the last half inch.

Some say we should be very specific in our prayers. To pray

for the exact job that we are looking for, for the precise amount in our bank account that would solve our financial troubles, for the perfect house we've always dreamed of owning, down to the brick patio.

I've prayed for many people I've never met face-to-face, people I've never known except by their email or Facebook requests, and I have to confess that the more specific the scenario, the easier it is to pray for them. Compassion comes with knowledge. When the woman writes about the scary cancer operation she's about to undergo and the struggles she's had to give up smoking and the Honda Accord in the garage that doesn't run very well, my heart goes out to her. The prayers come. I know who she is.

So much easier than when someone just puts down some initials: "Please remember A. B. and C. D. and F. G." Who are they? What's up with them? God might know, but I certainly don't. Which is pretty much what I say: *God, be with A. B. and C. D. and F. G.* I have to trust that's good enough. The thing is, all my fumbling attempts and halting efforts and last-ditch thoughts *are* good enough.

Trying is everything. It's the only way.

Part of me wants lists, a roll call of specific Bible readings, a roster of psalms to make my way through day after day. Indeed, the psalms have been part of my prayer practice for years. I used to have a pocket-sized Gideon Bible of the New Testament and Psalms and would turn to it on the subway. There was even a period when I would print out a psalm and carry it with me on my morning run. (You can imagine what a curious sight that made. "Why is that man reading a slip of paper as he runs?" Goodness knows.) I've listened to recordings of the Bible and inspirational podcasts while exercising.

The thing about such efforts is that they are very humbling. I'm filled with questions: *What does that psalm mean? What does that passage say? What was the psalmist thinking? How does it apply to me? Why has it been saved and sung for all these years?* The biggest mystery: *Why do I feel better for saying these psalms?* I don't feel like an expert for doing it. Just the opposite; I'm repeatedly made aware of how little I know. I close my eyes and shut everything out and concentrate on *God* or *love* or *faith* and trust that I'm becoming the person God wants me to become. I'm an amateur.

Prayer is a school for amateurs. An amateur is someone who does what they do for the love of doing it. In the case of prayer, practice doesn't make perfect; it just makes you know you are dependent on so much more than your own resources.

The mother of James and John came to Jesus with a special request. She wanted one son to sit at Jesus' left hand and one to sit at his right hand in God's kingdom. She wanted what many of us want, spiritual prestige, a step up, an open door, a first-class ticket to heaven with no layovers or long waits. "You don't know what you're asking!" Jesus said (Matthew 20:22 CEB). (She didn't; we don't.)

"Can you drink from the cup that I'm about to drink from?" Jesus asked. (What in the world would that be?) "We can," they said (v. 22 CEB). (How would they know? How would any of us know?)

"You will drink from my cup, but to sit at my right or left hand isn't mine to give," Jesus said. "It belongs to those for whom my Father prepared it" (v. 23 CEB).

I can laugh off the disciples' spiritual aspirations and cluck my tongue at their general cluelessness. What were they thinking? Hadn't they heard Jesus stress the power of servant-hood, that the first shall be last and the last shall be first? And yet, I have to admit I have my own such private yearnings. I want rewards, recognition, a halo for all to see. That seat at the right hand of the Father would certainly offer proof that I'm doing all the godly things.

One year I made enough trips, logged enough miles on one airline, and charged enough on its credit card that I was given exalted status. What did it get me? I was bumped up in the boarding process, able to get on board before the other economy travelers. Did I find it embarrassing to make my way to the front of the line? "Excuse me, that's my call." By all means. Did I give up the opportunity? Not a chance.

Some saint I'd make.

When the other disciples got wind of this special request to sit at Jesus' right and left hands, they were peeved. Jealous, no doubt. Why hadn't they thought to make such a request? Where would they be in the pecking order now?

"Whoever wants to be great among you will be your servant. Whoever wants to be first among you will be your slave," Jesus told them (vv. 26–27 CEB).

We can't do that by toadying to others, putting ourselves down, becoming Oscar worthy actors in bogus scenes of false modesty. We can't pretend to be who we aren't. We need to accept our gifts, acknowledge our strengths, confront our weaknesses, and become servants to others through our God-given callings. We can love people and prize them through our own sense of worthlessness.

When you're all alone in meditation and contemplative prayer, you can't weasel out of anything. You can't pass the buck. Challenging stuff is going to come up, times you didn't measure up to who you want to be. You might try to focus on all your successes, but your failures will speak out. Wrestling with them is worth every minute of it.

Humility is perhaps one of the most misunderstood of virtues. It's not pretending to be less, putting yourself in places where you are scorned and belittled. Please don't do that. Life is tough enough as it is. There's no need to pound your chest or scrape and bow. True humility is simpler and cleaner. Humility, as I've come to understand it, is acceptance. That cleansing attitude of, *Okay, God, I'm struggling here, in over my head. We'll get through this together somehow. Stay close to me. I need you. I can't do it all on my own. And I know you don't expect me to do it all on my own. Only with your help.* As Jesus said, "To sit at my right or left hand isn't mine to give. It belongs to those for whom my Father prepared it."

It is out of our hands.

There's a prayer that Eleanor Roosevelt said every night, according to her son: "Our Father, who has set a restlessness in our hearts and made us all seekers after that which we can never fully find, forbid us to be satisfied with what we make of life. Draw us from base content and set our eyes on far-off goals. Keep us at tasks too hard for us that we may be driven to Thee for strength."[2]

One line in particular has always moved me: *Tasks too hard for us that we may be driven to Thee for strength.* What could be more humbling than the model of Eleanor Roosevelt? What extraordinary things she accomplished, what challenges she faced to become the strong, affirming, visionary woman she was. Insecure, belittled, told that she was ugly from a young age, she was the daughter of a vain beauty of a mother and a raging alcoholic father. She might have been born into wealth and status, but it offered little reassurance and inner security. And yet she found her way forward, not without much struggle. *Forbid us to be satisfied with what we make of life. Set our eyes on far-off goals.* That's what a rich inner life can do: change the outer life.

My grandfather was not one of her fans, not by a long shot. He was a die-hard Republican, and for him she represented everything that had gone wrong in this country. Then one day he ended up sitting next to her on a long flight in those early days of commercial air travel, probably before the war. There he was, sitting next to a woman he reviled.

I have no idea what they discussed, but he ran a small construction business in Los Angeles, and according to her biographer, my friend David Michaelis, she was always interested in meeting American businessmen and finding out what they did and how it mattered to them, what challenges they faced.[3]

At any rate, by the end of the trip, my grandfather had fallen head over heels in love with her. He was won over. He found her absolutely charming and beautiful, inside and out. Not that she changed any of his political views, but the meeting changed how he saw her. It reversed everything. That's the power of true humility, in the best sense of the word.

Think of that when you are meditating and you're distraught that a million things are going through your mind. You become obsessed with all that seems to be going wrong in this world. You say your sacred word. You invoke a single syllable, like *God,* in the midst of your thoughts. You come back to stillness. And then your silly mind has taken you off to the races. You're upset by a comment someone made on social media. You're irritated by a story you read in the news. You can't abide the political scenery any longer. It pains you and makes you physically ill.

Perhaps it's your back that bothers you or your butt that's gone numb—you've just noticed that all of a sudden. There's an itch on your nose. (Scratch it.) Your phone buzzes in your pocket. (No, you don't need to look at that text. It can wait.) You start to think that you are the worst in the world at doing this meditating stuff, this sitting, this attempt at contemplative prayer. Why not give it up?

Welcome to the club. If I were a champion at it, if it came effortlessly to me, I don't think I'd be writing about it. I wouldn't have anything to say. I wouldn't know how hard it can be or what challenges we sainted sinners face. This struggle is the process, is the pleasure, is the practice. I can accept that God is working through me. My job is simply to put myself here in this sacred space, in this sacred time.

Remember that old saying, "The road to hell is paved with good intentions"? What nonsense. The road to heaven is paved with the best of intentions too.

My favorite of the three parts of Dante's *Divine Comedy* has always been the middle section, the part where the poet is in purgatory. Not hell, not heaven—*il paradiso*, as it's called in Italian—but *purgatorio*, the seven-story mountain that Thomas Merton referred to in the title of his momentous memoir.[4]

I don't believe in purgatory, a middle zone where most of us go after death to work off all our sins, spending count-less years, centuries, millennia scrambling up that mountain, getting to know ourselves, facing up to our faults, asking for God's forgiveness, until we can finally achieve the eternal bliss of paradise. But the idea of purgatory appeals to me as a metaphor for the spiritual journey we all undertake. I like the cosmic notion that what we start here on earth, what we aspire to, continues in the afterlife. The trajectory goes on. What we reach for, what we try to do, what we want to achieve and never quite make—it's all worth it because we are setting ourselves on the right direction for the forever part of our lives, that climb up Dante's mythical mountain. As the poet Robert Browning said, "A man's reach should exceed his grasp, or what's a heaven for?"[5]

As I said, intention is everything, especially in our prayers.

Think of the Canaanite woman who came to Jesus and shouted at him to get his attention. Her daughter was plagued by a demon, as she put it, and desperately needed healing. At first, he didn't answer her, and his followers urged him to avoid the woman, who was making a scene.

"I was sent only to the lost sheep of the house of Israel," Jesus said, apparently insulting her (Matthew 15:24). (Jesus sometimes said things that don't sound Jesus-like at all. It's as though he was calling attention to what he was about to do. His audience would have had their prejudices about this woman, and he seemed to be reminding them of that—just so they could fully take in how big his message was, that all are meant to be saved, not just people like them.)

The woman came to Jesus and knelt before him, saying, "Lord, help me" (v. 25).

He answered, "It is not right to take the children's bread and throw it to the dogs" (v. 26). Another insult. (Pay attention.)

She said, "Yes, Lord, yet even the dogs eat the crumbs that fall from their masters' table" (v. 27).

"Woman, great is your faith!" Jesus said. "Be it done for you as you desire" (v. 28).

Her daughter was healed instantly.

All those negative words, all that discouragement—she refused to hear it. She listened to the attacks and turned them around. *Even the dogs eat the crumbs that fall from their masters' table.* In the end, her humility was rewarded. Her doggedness came through.

To take another example, think of the woman who had been suffering for twelve years with a hemorrhage that no doctor could cure. She approached Jesus in the crowd and touched the fringe of his cloak. She didn't even have the courage to speak out. Understandably. In that culture and era, when menstruating women—let alone someone bleeding for twelve years—were excluded from worship, she would have been classified as an untouchable, not worthy. And yet her faith was such that she knew that touching the hem of Jesus' garment would be enough, more than enough.

Jesus felt the power leave him. He felt her faith. He didn't need words. Her faith was enough. He turned and saw her and told her, "Your faith has made you well" (Matthew 9:22). She was healed. She is the perfect model for prayer. No words were uttered. No scene was made. Just belief was shown. Just reaching out and touching something that had touched Jesus.

The gospel writers knew what they were doing putting these stories in their narratives. They were exalting the poor, the outcasts, the unnamed, the untouchables. These were the ones who understood who Jesus was in an instant, not the disciples, who often struggled to understand—even Peter, especially Peter.

How many times did Jesus have to tell Peter, "Feed my lambs" before he got it? How many times did Jesus have to ask the question, "Do you love me?" (John 21:15)? How many times does he have to ask *us*?

When people brought children to Jesus so he could lay his hands on them and pray, the disciples wanted them sent away. No, no, they had it all wrong, Jesus said. Let the children come to him. The kingdom of God belongs to *them*. Not necessarily because they are innocent and beguiling, as we like to think, but because they are like the lepers and the slaves and the Canaanite woman, low on the totem pole. This new world is for the likes of them.

And us.

Part of me wants to object. "Well, that's not me," I say. "I'm one of the lucky ones. I was born into a good family. My parents took me to church. I was baptized, loved, a prize student in Sunday school, a member of the choir. I am a congregant in good standing." But good standing means being a work in progress, keeping at it, never giving up, putting those intentions in prayer over and over again.

When I was in my early twenties and trying to figure out who I wanted to be and what I wanted to do in life, I became friends with an elderly woman. She was the widow of the minister who had baptized me, and she lived in a retirement home in Santa Barbara. I was there for the summer doing summer stock, performing night after night in a theater on a cliff overlooking the Pacific. Being the star of a musical would have seemed to be the fulfillment of my life's dream: standing on a stage, singing, my eye on the conductor in the pit, my heart in my throat, my nerves on edge, waiting for the reassuring applause at the end and a gratifying curtain call. I was a working actor. A star.

And I was miserable at it. This was not what I really wanted to do. But what did I want? Who did I want to become?

She took me to the retirement home for lunch, got me a singing gig at her church, and brought her companions from the home to hear me at the theater. Most of all, she modeled for me what faith in action was. One of the most selfless souls I was to ever know, she made caring about others a habit. It was such a habit that she didn't even know she was doing it.

As she spoke about her life and her marriage, I became aware that who she was wasn't an accident. She worked at it. She prayed at it. She set the intention in motion and she became what she wanted to be. She wouldn't have said that. She probably thought of herself as a work in progress. No matter; the lesson took. If I was going to become who I wanted to be, I needed to start right now, right then.

I'm still working at it.

Meditative Moment

Breathe a prayer.

At the very beginning when humans were made, our Creator breathed in us the breath of life. Every breath we take is a connection back to that. Use that in prayer.

Years ago, my friend David told me how he breathed in God's love. He'd close his eyes for a moment, picture God's love, and breathe it in. It was like eating a sweet pastry for breakfast. You could count if you want to, using the pranayama pattern 4-7-8: four seconds to inhale, seven seconds to hold the breath, eight seconds to exhale. But quite frankly, I'd rather use a word or two rather than a number: "God is love" or "God's love" or "Love, love, love."

Another prayer of intention is the Jesus Prayer—"Lord Jesus Christ, Son of God, have mercy on me"—which probably goes back to the Desert Fathers in the fifth century and has a rich heritage in the Eastern church. It is a way of praying without ceasing, putting yourself in relationship with God, and staying in that relationship through thick and thin.

Say it breathing in and repeat it breathing out, doing it as many times as you like.

Okay, now try saying either the Jesus Prayer or a short exclamation of "God's love." Breathe in, breathe out. Breathe in, breath out. A dozen times.

☩·☩·☩

Your cognitive self can be conscious of a prayer as it fills your unconscious. Praying with the breath is a deeply contemplative act. For me, with every breath I can feel God's Spirit say, I'm with you. You're with me. You're okay. You are loved.

chapter seven

Focus on Death

You might want to think about death. Although *want* is probably an exaggeration.

Our younger son, Tim, broke his femur in a tricycle accident at nursery school at age four. He had to be in traction in the hospital for twenty-six days, his leg up in the air. We had twenty-six days of trying to keep him distracted from his trapped state. "Like being stuck with your kid on an airplane for twenty-six days," his babysitter observed. We read, we drew pictures, we played games, we watched a big purple dinosaur on TV, we sang.

The day after Tim's accident, his older brother, William, came down with the chicken pox and had to be cared for at home. To fill out the full order of a triple whammy (why do these things come in threes?), I had a tumor on my parotid gland that needed to be excised right away. I was scheduled for surgery while Tim was in the hospital. My doctor reassured me—holding up one finger to silence my worries—that the tumor didn't look to be malignant. Still, it had to come out.

My wife, Carol, and I had been taking turns at Tim's hospital bed, spending alternate nights sleeping on a cot in his room. The night before surgery I slept there, listening to a four-year-old toss and turn in the never-completely-dark and never-completely-quiet stillness of a hospital at night. *If I die*, I thought to myself, *this is exactly what I would want to be doing in the last moments of my life. Spending time with my son.* (I would also have liked it if William and Carol were there too.)

Later I shared the thought in a letter to my friend Claire Townsend. Claire had been a figure of considerable glamour in college, three years above me. A trailblazer, she was one of the first class of women undergrads admitted to Princeton. She had interned for Ralph Nader one summer; sang in the Triangle Club, the musical-comedy club on campus; then moved out to Hollywood, where she ended up making a name for herself as a vice president at 20th Century Fox.[1] There our paths crossed again when, in a brief foray, I was looking for work as an actor-singer—a career path I soon abandoned.

At the time she, too, was making a life change, going from Hollywood exec to spiritual seeker. She turned up one Sunday at a forum at the church I attended in Pasadena to discuss her journey and the paucity of spiritual content in Hollywood films—no surprise there. We talked a bit then and stayed in touch. She soon quit Hollywood, studied law, took up a spiritual practice, and made a documentary about Peace Pilgrim, a woman who gave up all worldly goods back in the fifties and spent the rest of her life walking around the United States, proclaiming peace.[2]

We often discussed our prayer lives. I remember one example she gave, from when she was a Hollywood exec, of her silently "shooting love," as if from a *Star Wars* lightsaber, at her colleagues during a particularly contentious meeting and seeing things calm down and become more creative. Would that I could do as much. She read an early draft of my first spiritual memoir, *Finding God on the A Train*, and gave me helpful feedback. She was wise, funny, thoughtful, smart—and dying. At the time she had been diagnosed with breast cancer and was getting treatments. I assumed she would recover, like so many cancer sufferers. She died the next year at age forty-three.

We live, we die, we pray, we meditate. Claire, of all people, knew what it meant to get a scary diagnosis and how important it was to treasure every minute, not just for this life but for the next, whatever that would be. Spending the night on a cot next to my son on a hospital bed was a worthwhile thing to do. It was as though I had focused one of those lightsabers of love and was shooting it at myself, right in the heart. All would be well. God would be with us.

I went into surgery the next day—at a different hospital than my son's—feeling ready, spiritually prepared. Did I say a few prayers before they put me out with anesthesia? Of course I did. For me, for my family, for the doctors working on me.

I woke up many hours later in a recovery room, feeling awful. Not prayerful at all. The surgery was supposed to be an outpatient procedure, meaning I would go home afterward. But removing the tumor had taken a long time, longer than the surgeon expected. He had to extract it without injuring any of the threadlike facial nerves wrapped around it. My face was stunned in the process, and I discovered that I couldn't move half of it. I couldn't smile on my left side, couldn't wink. I had to close one eye manually.

No, I would not go home that afternoon. I spent the night at the hospital, and the next day a young resident bandaged me up, swathing me in tape and gauze. I looked like an extra from a film about the Civil War, one of the walking wounded.

What I wondered, what had me stumped, was this: Where had all that meditative serenity gone? Why couldn't I access the divine now? Why couldn't I accept that this misery was just part of the journey of life? I could tell myself I was grateful for the doctors' good care, but I didn't feel it at all. When I closed my eyes—manipulating one eye by hand—all I accessed was the calm-shattering shock of anesthesia and surgery. And the fear of death.

It was my introduction to the challenge medical disasters bring to a prayer life. I understood why a woman like Claire, a person with probing faith and a dedicated spiritual practice, could also be afraid when dealing with breast cancer. When you need to practice meditation the most is often when it's hardest.

Certain assumptions, spoken or unspoken, accompany most medical procedures and treatments. The doctors are going to make you well, the treatment—no matter its crippling side effects—will heal you. The drugs will save you. The surgery will cure what ails you. No one likes to bring up how you might feel in the process. No one tells you beforehand that your head, no matter what they do to your body, will not be in the same place it was. At least it wasn't for me.

A dozen years after that benign tumor was removed—yes, it was benign—I had to undergo open-heart surgery for an aortic aneurysm, the result of a bicuspid valve I was born with (oh, the bounty in our genes). This was a big deal, no walk in the park. The surgeon was the most confident—dare I say arrogant?— creature on earth. Yes, you want confidence in a surgeon. You want the person to know what he or she is doing. Maybe it takes just that kind of cockiness to cut someone up, to take the patient's life in your gloved hands. Still, it doesn't address how a patient feels.

"I'll fix you up," he said, "and you'll go on living your life." But what kind of life would it be? How would it change? How would I change? After some cardiac rehab sessions at the hospital, I would eventually go back to jogging in the park, my patched-up heart doing its job efficiently. But how would the heart of my emotional life be?

We were scheduled to go to Spain for a vacation four weeks after the surgery. "No problem," said the surgeon. "You'll be just fine. All fixed up."

We did not go to Spain.

For months afterward, whenever I closed my eyes to slip into meditative prayer, I found myself in a dark box. The black domino, I called it. I'm not sure why. Maybe it was because I felt trapped in blackness or on the curve of a row of soldierlike dominos where all of us would fall down. All it would take was one push.

I don't doubt that some of it was clinical. Depression can be a side effect of open-heart surgery. Not that I seemed listless or lost. On the contrary, I felt overly alert, wary. It was hard to fall asleep at night. It was as though my body were saying, *I'm not going to do that again. Remember when you fell asleep in the OR and they ripped open your sternum and cut you up? Don't let someone do that to you again.*

Hospitals save countless lives. Western medicine is its own miracle. But its good work can thrash a soul, especially when we avoid the inevitability of death. In its focus on fixing people up, Western medicine often avoids confronting our mortality.

I once met a woman who worked as a hospital chaplain in an oncology ward. She became aware that one of the challenges she faced was the high burnout rate of the staff. Every day they were dealing with life-and-death matters with the hope, the intention, the goal of preserving life. It wasn't always possible. Patients died, despite their best efforts.

She instigated a new procedure: when a patient died,

instead of immediately moving on, the staff would gather in the patient's room and have a moment of silence. To share in the sorrow and wonder of what had happened, to know it, to take it in, to not simply run away from it and get on with business. To face the truth. Death is part of life. Know it.

That is one of the goals of my meditative prayer practice. Jesus healed, Jesus cured, Jesus raised people from the dead, but when he faced the prospect of his own terrible death, when he prayed in the garden for this cup of suffering to be taken from him, he was not reassured. He had to pray that harder, deeper prayer, "Not my will, but thine, be done" (Luke 22:42 KJV).

How do lesser mortals like us do as much?

First of all, listen to the fears. Take them in as you sit silently in meditation. That ache in your chest, does it mean something worse than a little indigestion? Is that what your head is saying? That maddening throbbing in your head, is it something more than can be corrected with a dose of aspirin? That person who died in the accident luridly described in today's news, couldn't that be you? She was as innocent as you, but she crossed the street at the wrong moment, meeting a driver who was blinded by the morning light. No reason it couldn't be you. Hear your worries rumbling through you, the ones you would altogether rather avoid. (In meditation we meet the unavoidable.)

My friend the *New Yorker* cartoonist Roz Chast once published a scathing and brilliantly accurate picture of a man reading the obituaries. "Two Years Younger Than You," "Exactly Your Age," "Twelve Years Older Than You," "Your Age on the Dot," went the various captions.[3] Obituaries are *memento mori* if there ever were ones, reminders of death in cold type put down where they can't be argued with or shrugged off. But we do indeed try to shrug them off. Personally, I hate using the word *passed* instead of *died*. A death, when it happens, should be called by its name.

It is a good and righteous thing to know that death is always around the corner. A friend who knew more about saints than I do liked to tell the story—surely apochryphal—of the saintly Padre Pio, a man who was the vehicle of many of a miracle. Once he was asked by a fawning fan, "Oh Father Pio, what do you have to say to a woman who has just turned fifty?"

"Death is not far behind," he said mordantly.

Any minute on this earth could be our last. When I meditate in the morning on my subway commute, my concentration becomes more acute through those last three stations. "Canal Street . . . Chambers Street . . . Fulton Street," the conductor calls out. I know I'm going to have to get off soon—the clock is ticking, the train moving, my focus narrowing. My mind goes into a dark tunnel and the distracting thoughts go quiet. I land in a cloud of unknowing and time stretches out.

To be aware of the end is to know how transitory life is, to know that it should be savored. I'll have to get off the train soon. The exit ramp—to mix metaphors—is right around the corner.

In Jesus' time people lived closer to nature. You hear it in his parables. They knew that the seed must die for the flower to bloom. The wheat had to be cut and brought into harvest. No animal lived forever. No person did either. How magnificent that our life expectancy has been extended beyond the biblical "threescore years and ten" (Psalm 90:10 KJV).[4] Today if someone dies at seventy, you hear people say, "They seemed so young" (no matter how good and rich a life it had been). Pity those, though, who think they can avoid death forever and come up with elaborate plans to recycle their body parts endlessly, going for eternal life that way. Maybe they fantasize about being put in a Deepfreeze to be revived at some later date, a sci-fi resurrection. Anything to escape the final curtain. Jesus' message couldn't be realized *until* he died. Nor can we realize the beauty of our lives without accepting death. Resurrection—change—doesn't happen without it.

It's hard because we're so good at ignoring death, part of a culture that encourages our willful ignorance. For that very reason, it can come as a shock when thoughts of death make themselves known in meditation. The angel of death will flutter into a quiet moment, begging to be recognized. *Where did* she *come from?* we wonder. *Why is* he *here?*

Why? Because this is a place to bump against the truth that death *isn't* far behind.

Make meditation your friend when you're up against a medical challenge. Pray for others when they face such challenges. Share their fears, knowing that sense of mortality. "I hope with daring courage that Christ's greatness will be seen in my body," Paul wrote to the Philippians, "now as always, whether I live or die. Because for me, living serves Christ and dying is even better. If I continue to live in this world, I get results from my work. But I don't know what I prefer. I'm torn between the two because I want to leave this life and be with Christ, which is far better" (1:20–23 CEB).

Prayers of healing can also be prayers of acceptance.

Many of our medical establishments, the big hospitals and medical centers, owe their existence to religious institutions. NewYork-Presbyterian Hospital is only fifteen blocks away from our house—*Presbyterian* lingering in the name like a fading flower. In New York there is also Mount Sinai, St. Luke's, Beth Israel, Maimonides. On most mornings I run by an apartment complex that used to be St. Elizabeth's Hospital (next to the shrine of the immigrant saint Mother Cabrini). At NewYork-Presbyterian there is an old sign engraved in stone above a door that proclaims, "Healing Comes from the Most High." (A psychiatrist friend tells me that when he was a resident there, his fellow doctors joked this was the perfect excuse for getting stoned after work.)

These places had their origins at a time when religious orders and churches and synagogues were closely affiliated with healing. Over time, many hospitals loosened any holy alliance, not simply because that made more sense in running a medical business but also, I suspect, because religion lost its confidence in its own healing arts. Western medicine, with new surgeries and treatments, was doing such a good job on its own. Who needed that old-fashioned religion?

The falling away of the partnership was a loss for both parties. As I've said, there is a lot that happens to the spirit during a medical intervention that doctors, for all their gifts, are unprepared to address. Fortunately, in recent years, many hospitals are indeed reaching out to yoga teachers, Reiki experts, and hypnotists, not to mention providing chaplains to every ward. My friends who are chaplains offer witness to how much their ministry, full of prayers with not only a patient but family and friends, is treasured. Collaborators in healing of the spirit, if not the body and mind.

Teresa of Ávila (1515–1582), that tetchy spiritual mentor of yore, is famous for her down-to-earth pronouncements like "God save us from gloomy saints" or her outburst to God at a testy moment, "If this is how you treat your friends, no wonder you have so few of them."[5]

In one book she compared prayer to channeling water into two basins. In one case, the basin is filled by water that comes directly from the source; in the other, it comes via a series of man-made conduits. "The latter corresponds to the spiritual sweetness which [. . .] is produced by meditation. It reaches us by way of the thoughts; we meditate upon created things and fatigue the understanding; and when at last, by means of our own efforts, it comes, the satisfaction which it brings to the soul fills the basin."[6]

It would be ideal to have our basin directly connected to God, but there is also something wonderful—spiritual sweetness, she calls it—in the work of meditation, especially, in my favorite line, when we have managed to "fatigue the understanding." One of the pleasures of reading Teresa of Ávila is that indeed I don't understand her all the time—as I don't always understand where my contemplative prayers are going—but I feel happy in her presence and know her to be a companionable soul.

There is mystery in healing and mystery in suffering. It's logical to think that the suffering must have been greater in Teresa of Ávila's days—or certainly in biblical times—before we knew what we know today about germs and the power of modern medicine. But just because we can extend a life and bring physical healing through surgery, drugs, chemotherapy, or radiation doesn't mean we can save a soul from the emotional and psychological suffering that comes with serious illness. Facing the real prospect of death can be painful. In our wildernesses today, despite the connections we make through social media, there is uncounted loneliness and despair and a cosmic avoidance of death.

No wonder Jesus called upon us to visit the sick and the lonely. In one of his loveliest parables he reminded us that in visiting them, the least of these, we would be visiting him. Losing our lives in our love for others to find our true selves again. A plaque outside the nursing home where my father spent his final days said simply, "I was sick and you came to me," and we did. Not just for him but for *us*.

In the last week of my father's life, when he could no longer speak, when he had stopped eating and drinking, when the hospice nurse visited regularly, when we all agreed that he would not have wanted to be rushed off to the hospital if there were some dramatic cause, when we could reflect on the beauty of his life, when we could laugh at some of the things we had done with him, when we could rub his feet and squeeze his hands—up to the point where he couldn't squeeze them back—we all knew that we were in a sacred place, despite the commercials blaring on his roommate's TV. These last moments were moments we could treasure. What a loss it would have been if we couldn't have admitted to ourselves and to those who visited that he was dying. He was the least of these. We were the least of these.

If a chaplain had walked in and offered prayer—and I'm sure one did—it wouldn't have been an intrusion. We were already there. With every faltering breath he took, with the slowing of his heart rate, with the hands that didn't even squeeze back when we held them.

He didn't choose to die while we were there. But then he was always among the last to leave a party. Why not savor those final moments on earth, especially with your family at your bedside? Finally, on his last day, Mom stood at the foot of his bed—Mom, who had been the best of caregivers—and said, "Daddy, it's time to go." In due time, in his time, in God's time. In the middle of the night, when none of his four children or his wife or his grandchildren or his daughters- or sons-in-law were around, he left this world.

From the long, rambling graces we had heard him say at the dinner table, we knew he didn't believe that this world was the only world out there. From the many visits I had made with him to the cemetery where his parents and his beloved sister and his numerous aunts and uncles were buried, I knew that he knew death could be a friend, his companion. His own mother had died in that cemetery on a sun-drenched May day nearly fifty years earlier while visiting the graves of her loved ones, bringing them flowers.

The flowers don't last. Neither do we. Hold that in your prayers.

Meditative Moment

Here's a really quick exercise.
Don't linger at it.

You're going to meditate for only one minute. Set a timer for it. Imagine that this is the only chance you'll have for meditation all day. Things will be hectic. There will be countless demands on your time. All you have is this precious minute.

Find a place where no interruptions can stop

you. Go into a huddle room at the office. Go into your bedroom. Go into the proverbial closet that Jesus talks about.

Close your eyes or let them go at half-mast. Stare at something that won't change. No looking out at a beautiful scene for this exercise. You want deadly dull. No distractions. (This is why I prefer to close my eyes, because I always find something I want to stare at.)

Take a glance at nothingness. See a blank screen in front of a blank screen. This is your only chance. One minute of nothing. No talking to yourself. No listening to any meditation guides. Inner silence. Go.

How was it? Did you find that because of the pressure of limited time, you focused harder on the nothingness? You didn't want to risk losing it. The clock was ticking.

Life is like that. The clock is ticking. The days are piling up. The legendary UCLA basketball coach John Wooden used to say, "Make each day your masterpiece."[7] You can improve on what you did yesterday. You can dream about tomorrow. But today is it. This is the time you've got, the time the good Lord gave us. Your masterpiece. To know that we are all going to die is to know that we have only a few brief moments to make a difference, to be who we are. Confronting our mortality is crucial.

Use a quick sixty-second or thirty-second meditation whenever you want. When you're sitting at your computer, when you're on the phone and put on hold waiting for a customer service person to help you, when you're going over a pile of bills, when you're scrolling through too many emails. Close out, just for a brief while. You know you have to make the time count because it's so brief. Look what Jesus did in a few short years of ministry.

Death is a gift. Life is precious. We find beauty in the most transitory things—a sunset, the last rose of summer, autumn leaves, a snowfall. If they didn't change, we wouldn't treasure them so much. Fleeting is beautiful.

chapter eight

Look at the Images in Your Head

U se visual imagery to help you. Picture this:

When I step into meditative prayer, the sweet spot I look for, the comfort zone I like to land in, is something I'd more readily describe with visual imagery rather than any of the other senses. It's a place in my head—it feels like an actual location, a dark shelf on a bookcase toward the top or the bottom. I can feel my mind go lie there. I don't choose where it wants to go; all I know is it looks for rest, and rest is a place in my head that I can almost see.

I recall the story of an elderly man, the friend of a friend, in his last days. When my friend visited him at the hospital, he wanted to give her tea, like he had in his antique-laden apartment. He couldn't see what he needed in the bland hospital room. Instead, he closed his eyes and pictured what he wanted. He pointed to the spot where the teakettle could be found and the drawer where the tea leaves were stored. Could she get them down? Then there were the cups and saucers. Maybe she could get them, too, along with some milk from the fridge and a couple of silver spoons and the sugar bowl.

Close your eyes. Can't you picture a multitude of things? Can't you find something in your imagination that is impossible to see with your eyes open? The inner eye can see what the outer eye can't.

I have friends who prefer to meditate with their eyes open. They pick something to stare at: a spot on the wall, a piece of dust, a wrinkle in a pillow, a corner of a picture, a tile on the floor, faded wainscoting, a crack in the plaster, flaking paint. They find it easier to tune out that way, getting lost in a sight.

There is a rich ecclesiastical tradition of using icons—holy images—to focus on in prayer. We can get lost in the eyes of Jesus, stare at the mother Mary holding her baby. One of my favorites is the whole Trinity in one picture, the Father God holding the Son with the descending dove of the Holy Spirit casting rays down on the scene. In the Eastern tradition, the icon isn't simply a picture of what it represents; it is a living image. God is there. Does that seem so impossible? Isn't what we see in our mind's eye sometimes more real than the real thing?

In the back of our church there is a large framed painting of Jesus on the cross, a half-naked, life-size Christ with dreadlocks. He looks like a guy you'd see in the neighborhood, waiting for coffee at Starbucks or hurrying to get on the subway before the doors closed. An Armenian woman of much faith—and little English—used to come into the church during the day and stand leaning against the painting, her face on the glass almost touching Jesus', eye to eye, nose to nose. She would stay there for a long time, presumably praying. You didn't want to disturb her, but you'd gladly sign up for what she had.

I'm not fond of sentimentalized saintliness. You know, like when people say, "Get her to pray for you. She's got a direct line to heaven." We all have a direct line to heaven. We simply have to trust it. Take a risk and run with it.

This woman had come from a tradition of icons and knew how to use them. Even though the painting is distinctly modern, influenced by Western artistic tradition—there's nothing other-worldly about those dreadlocks and that tortured expression on Jesus' face—she treated it as an icon, physically embracing it, her head pressed against Jesus. You can't ever tell what is going through someone's head when he or she is deep in contemplative prayer. Maybe she was just going over her marketing list for the bodega or figuring out what to buy for Christmas for her grandchildren. Maybe she was reviewing the schedule of Sunday services. (There are enough times when I'm in the midst of prayer that the Google calendar inserts itself into my view.) Once though, after she had left, our pastor went up to the painting and noticed drops of moisture on the glass where she had put her face. What the woman saw in her mind's eye had moved her to tears.

Let me mention a personal moment with that image. On a weekday, the church was being used for the annual blood drive. The chair where you sat to donate blood was at the front of the sanctuary staring back to that portrait. A beloved family member found herself reflecting on Christ offering his own blood. I can never see that painting without feeling the same connection. Yes, Christ, you did this for us. What can we do for you?

"Christ has no body now but yours. No hands, no feet on earth but yours," says a prayer attributed to Teresa of Ávila. "Yours are the eyes through which he looks compassion on this world. Yours are the feet with which he walks to do good. Yours are the hands through which he blesses all the world. Yours are the hands, yours are the feet, yours are the eyes, you are his body. Christ has no body now on earth but yours." It was as though that Armenian woman, now deceased, was crying in compassion over what Jesus suffered, feeling the suffering herself.

There was a recent show at the Frick museum of paintings

by the Late Renaissance artist Giovanni Battista Moroni, a lesser-known contemporary of Titian's. He's been a favorite of my wife's and mine ever since we first encountered him in Bergamo on our honeymoon. He's best known for his portraits, vivid images of the titled and well-dressed as well as more humble folk, such as a tailor standing at a worktable,[1] from his corner of northern Italy. One woman stares out at the viewer in a dress with gold brocade, a jeweled cross at her neck and a marten fur on her shoulder.[2] A knight in a silk doublet with a sword at his side has a light beard and mustache that would go over well in a Brooklyn bar. He stands in front of an image of the prophet Elijah ascending to heaven on his chariot, letting his cloak fall to his successor, Elisha (perhaps a reference to a passing on of the torch for the knight?).[3]

In one corner of the gallery were three more-subdued portraits, notables in dark clothes with scenes of saints in a blue sky above them. The caption explained that these were references to the Spiritual Exercises of St. Ignatius of Loyola, where practitioners are instructed to meditate on episodes in Christ's life, using all five senses to put themselves in the scene. Moroni used only one sense, sight, to show what his sitters were contemplating. A middle-aged couple, one of them holding a prayer book, is in front of a Virgin and child floating on clouds, with a few angels peeking out from under Mary's feet and the archangel Michael carrying the three-pronged scales of justice for the Virgin—and the couple—to observe.[4] Moroni showed us their meditative practice. It's not just what they aspire to; it's the work they do.

As a writer and occasional teacher of writing, I often emphasize how readers don't necessarily linger over the magic of words on the page as much as they see images in their heads of what the writer has been telling them. Vivid pictures scroll through the brain as they read, a cinema in the head. Even when a masterful novelist like Edith Wharton has a character go into a long inner monologue, she sets the scene with enough details so you can see where the character is and what they're doing when they are nursing all those profound thoughts. Readers remember pictures more than they remember sentences. The Bible is an especially interesting case when you consider that for many centuries, most people simply heard its words. Few could afford to own a precious manuscript copy. Even monks in monasteries—unless they were copyists—depended on hearing the words read aloud. They listened with the mind's eye.

They, like us, created pictures in their heads of what they heard. The stories of Jesus unfolded in their imaginations. Inspired by the Exercises, the subjects in the Moroni portraits meditated by putting themselves in the scenes they envisioned. No reason we can't do the same, immersing ourselves in a vivid, living Bible.

I'm envious of those blessed souls who can quote long passages of Scripture, chapter and verse, at the drop of a hat. I need the words to be set to music to stick in my head. (I had to sing my ABCs for years before I could ever recite them.) When I think of the Bible, I see scenes: Moses parting the Red Sea, Jesus walking on water, Adam and Eve in the garden, Daniel in the lions' den, the baby in the manger, Jesus breaking the bread, Paul accosted on the road to Damascus, Christ ascending to heaven. (The latter has been underscored by one of my favorite paintings at the Met museum that shows only his feet at the top of the canvas with the disciples looking up.)[5]

When I turn to the Bible in meditation, if a picture forms in my head, I'll focus on closing my eyes and seeing the scene.

In his parables Jesus gave us images to connect to. The lost coin, the pearl beyond price, the lost sheep, the sheep and the goats, the house that stood on the firm foundation. I've never met a shepherd, but I have a very clear picture of what it's like to have a lost sheep, thanks to Jesus.

In one of the parables, Jesus slogged through the basics of farming. A farmer was sowing seed. Some seeds fell on the path, and the birds came and ate them. Some fell on rocky ground with no depth of soil. Seedlings sprang up quickly, but with nowhere for the roots to grow, they withered and died. Other seeds fell among thorns, and when they came up, the thorns choked and killed them. But there was some seed that landed in good soil, and it dug into the ground and grew up, multiplying thirty, sixty, a hundred times. The practice of meditation is to turn ourselves into good soil. We dig up the rocks, tossing them aside. We root out the thorns and weeds, cutting them back. We watch out for the birds, lest they rob us of our good work. We look to the seeds we have planted in ourselves or that have taken root there through the loving ministration of others. We see them grow like magic, spreading their branches, blossoming, multiplying, giving us shade, bearing fruit, making new seeds. We don't know how it happened, but it did, and we are grateful. All we did was take care of ourselves, nurturing the soil.

"Faith is the gift of God. But you can ask for this gift," James William Kimball wrote.[6] That is the paradoxical nature of belief. We work at it—you have to work at it—but at the same time, we receive it as if there were no work at all. There is a tendency, as I've said, to stress the no-work part of that gift. We want people to know that God is present and available. We want them to be enveloped in God's love, free for the taking. And yet without taking care of our soil—without tilling it, watering it, weeding it, digging in, turning it over, patting it down—that gift can take flight faster than the birds. To pray is the easiest thing on the earth. And to make sure you have the habit of putting yourself in God's presence is the work of a lifetime. It only makes sense if you do it day after day after day.

Fortunately, over the years, I've met people who are models of prayer for me and keep me at it. Take my friend Debbie, a very successful novelist. A tireless worker, she has written more books than even she can count and has sold more than I can count. But we weren't talking about writing books; we were talking about the habit of prayer. She gets up even earlier than I do, at 4:30 in the morning, to read the Bible and write in her journals—including a gratitude journal in which she records at least five things a day that she is thankful for—and pray. Many people ask her to pray for them, and she remembers them. She prays for herself, for her work, for her family. She meditates on whatever she has read that morning in a handful of devotional books. She's been doing this for decades. It's how she starts her day, no matter where she is, even when she's on vacation. She tills the soil.

"Do you ever take a day off?" someone asked her.

Yes, she does. If she has to skip a day for some reason or other, she will. "But only one day," she says. "You can't skip two days." *You can't skip two days.*

Habits are habit-forming. Stick to them and they only become easier. If you can only give meditation five minutes a day of your precious time, do it five minutes a day *every day.*

The "every day" is more important than how long it is. The power is in the practice. You will find that you don't want to be without the practice of sitting in darkness that brings you light, the savoring of silence that gives you the power to turn off life's brutal noise.

Be the soil. It's so much easier than turning yourself into a seed.

Let me try another image here. It comes from a painting— and from the Bible. I have long been a fan of the work of the artist Henry Ossawa Tanner (1859–1937).[7] His father was a bishop in the African Methodist Episcopal Church; his mother had been born into slavery in Virginia but escaped to the North through the Underground Railroad. He grew up in Philadelphia and was a student at the Pennsylvania Academy of the Fine Arts, where some of his finest paintings are hung. He spent most of his career in Paris where, as an African American, he found it easier to work and to be accepted, especially being married to a white woman (the model for Mary in more than one of his paintings). Once on a visit to New York City, while he was walking with his son, he realized that people assumed he was the boy's servant.

He painted some powerful genre scenes, but after trips to the Holy Land in the 1890s, he devoted himself almost entirely to biblical scenes. He subtracted the gloss of religious conventions and went into the heart of a story. His biblical characters look like real people; the settings were often drawn from his travels in the Middle East.

At the Pennsylvania Academy of the Fine Arts, in one of those skylit galleries enveloped in natural light, paintings are hung in a nineteenth-century fashion, some two or three or four deep, covering a whole wall. There is—blessedly—a bench in the center so you can sit and take them in, over time. You can meditate on them, staring at them as if gazing at icons, losing yourself to find yourself. How long can you look at a painting? As long as it takes, as long as you like.

On one wall is Tanner's *Nicodemus*, his portrait of the Pharisee meeting with Jesus under the veil of night.[8] Nicodemus has made the trip under the cover of darkness for fear of being recognized as a seeker and not the know-it-all Pharisee he was expected to be. The Pharisees get a bad rap in the Bible, but I think they're there to remind us how we can all be Pharisees. Get me into a political discussion and I will shock myself by my Pharisee-like sureness in argumentation, the narrow-mindedness, the arrogance, my absolute unwillingness to do what Jesus asked, which was to love my neighbor—nay, love my enemy.

There in Tanner's painting is Nicodemus on a Judean roof-top, meeting Jesus one-on-one—the best way to meet anyone, when you're free from posturing, free from the tyranny of what others might think about you or what you fear they might know about you. The light in Tanner's painting is fabulous; the source at first seems to be lamplight or firelight coming up a flight of stairs, illuminating Jesus as he looks lovingly, understandingly, at Nicodemus. Then you realize that the light is also coming from Jesus himself.

(I knew a lighting designer who, in an exercise in school, was asked to re-create the lighting of a Rembrandt painting, using models and fabric and every bit of sophisticated lighting that was available at the school. He couldn't do it. It couldn't be done. The lighting only existed on the canvas.)

I'd seen reproductions of the *Nicodemus* painting before but was seeing it now in the flesh, the real thing, every brushstroke visible if I got up close. I did and then sat back down to meditate, getting lost in the imagery. I could hear Jesus telling Nicodemus that he had to be born again, born anew, and how mystifying that was to Nicodemus. To be born of the Spirit—the light coming up the stairs and the light coming from Jesus. There was the Spirit. Other art viewers came into the gallery, looked at some of the paintings, then left. I stayed, not counting the time, letting myself enjoy a picture that I had always loved but now was seeing for the first time. Allowing myself to feel like Nicodemus, born anew. I didn't look at my watch or check my phone. I just stared at the painting.

A friend was telling me about seeing a famous artist at one of those large retrospective exhibits that encompasses room after room in a museum and attracts huge crowds. The famous artist was in one of the first galleries, staring at a masterpiece. My friend noticed him and then moved on. At the end of her tour through the exhibit a good hour later, she came back to that first room. The famous artist was still there, taking in that single painting. It deserved that. It gave up its secrets or revealed new ones with time.

I've mentioned using a single-syllable word like *God* in your meditation. Using a single image is okay too. Go with whatever it is. Stay with the same thing. Try something different. Try nothing.

There are plenty of apps and videos out there with guided meditations. Use them. See if they help you with scenes and scenarios that take you out of yourself. I find that the best images, the most profound, are ones that simply drop into my head without any prompting, like images from a dream. Do I see my mind lying on a shelf? No, but as I practice letting go, as I mutter a one-syllable word like *God*, the dark quietness of that place will appear, the place where my mind must rest, the comfort of unknowing.

It's like when Paul said, "For we do not know how to pray as we ought, but that very Spirit intercedes with sighs too deep for words" (Romans 8:26 NRSV). Images can take us beyond words. Here's one I find I use a lot, especially when I'm falling asleep at night. I picture a glowing ember, like a fire in a fireplace, warming the heart. God's love, God's power, watching over me, keeping me at peace.

Meditative Moment
Make your own movie.

As you sit on your pillow or chair or sofa, create a movie in your head. Not a violent, on-the-edge-of-your-seat thriller but a plotless, meandering play-by-play that no one else would want to watch. It should put them to sleep. Boring for them, engaging for you.

Give yourself an image. A path in the woods, wind blowing across a lake, a flower, a tree, a beach, a mountain, a field, a stream. A beloved family member, a room that harbors deep memories—I'm pulling up a classroom at the church of my childhood—a teacher, a friend, Jesus. Hold the image for a few seconds. Let it scroll to another image.

Don't talk to the image; don't make it talk to you. Let it be a quiet prayer.

This exercise is not visualization, as such. It's almost the opposite. You're not visualizing any sort of answer to prayer. Rather you're scrolling through images that put you in touch with the imageless Creator. You're finding the God within. Less here is more.

One of the ones I like is emptiness. What did the women see first on Easter morning? An empty tomb. It makes me think that emptiness is what prepares us to see and confront that holiest image of all, the resurrection.

You could look for images in advance. Thumb through a book; search a subject on Google and scroll through the images. Pick what you like. I find my imagination delivers plenty of visuals. Nothing very fancy; sometimes just a corner of a rock, a piece of cloth, a patch of grass. Let them come to you very naturally. Go for it. Don't make it work. Let it be godly play.

✛·✛

The two disciples on that long walk to Emmaus didn't even recognize the risen Christ until they invited him to stay with them. Then Jesus broke the bread. Their eyes were opened. And in that same instant, he was gone. All they had was what they held in their heads.

chapter nine

Put Away Your Phone (Every Now and Then)

L et's talk frankly about our phones.

   I love my cell phone. I love the way it connects me with the world. I treasure being able to communicate with my wife, my family, and my friends through quick texts. It's so great that someone can send you a picture—a picture worth more than a thousand words—and you can respond to it in seconds. I check the news. I like scrolling through all those great images on Instagram. I'm glad I can keep up with emails almost anywhere. I love being able to FaceTime someone, seeing the person I'm talking to. I like having a whole bunch of apps at my fingertips. I've used a Bible app and a prayer app and one for the daily office, with readings for the day. Better than having to lug books around in my backpack. It's all there on my phone—easy to read, accessible, and so much cheaper than in the old days of making calls on landlines. I remember the dark ages when you had to make phone calls at certain times of day just because it was cheaper. I remember calling home and hanging up after two rings—a signal to Mom and Dad that they were supposed to call me back. "It's your dime," we said, or "your nickel." No dimes or nickels clocking the ticking minutes anymore.

   Long distance isn't the burden it once was with things like Skype. We have plans that give us hours of use. Most plans offer unlimited mobile-to-mobile calling.

   Phones are great. And they're also not so great.

   Phones can take us away from where we are. Talk about not

being present. Someone's phone will buzz, and they'll check it to see who called, or they'll answer an email or text—just for a moment. All at once they are out of the room. They might think they're there, but they're not. I know when I do it, I'm miles and miles away. You can't do two things at once. Not well. You can't text one person while listening to another. You can't read an email from one contact while pretending to hear what someone else is saying. You can't be two places at once. (There were saints back in holy times who could do that, but I haven't met anyone today who can do the same—even with the magic of a cell phone.)

I've always figured I wasn't addicted to my phone. I depended on it, yes. Referred to it and checked it, but not all the time. The average person spends over five hours a day on their phone.[1] I'm a little bit below that (according to my phone). But heck, some of that time was devoted to a podcast I listened to while I worked out at the gym. That doesn't count, right?

One day I left my phone at work. I was phoneless for thirteen, maybe fourteen hours. What a disaster. I couldn't text my wife to tell her that the subway was running with delays. Couldn't read the latest news to distract myself during those delays. Couldn't text one of my late-working colleagues at the office and ask her to see if my phone was on my desk. I couldn't listen to a podcast in the morning when I went for a run. Couldn't check the weather. Couldn't scroll through photos at breakfast. Couldn't catch up with emails on the way to work. Couldn't know who was trying to get ahold of me. Couldn't distract myself with social media. Couldn't get on my favorite Bible app.

Distract is an interesting word. Why should we feel the need for distraction? Distract us from what? Aren't there things out there that are meant to be seen? Aren't we supposed to pay attention? How can I be aware if I'm looking for distraction? I wanted to believe that my spiritual practice lessened my need for distraction. I go into meditation, leaving the world behind so that I can pay it the right attention when I open my eyes. But this cell phone attachment seemed to prove me wrong.

After that I decided I'd go on a cell phone fast. Heck, it was Lent. If there was a time for a cell phone fast, wasn't this it? I wasn't going to give the phone up for forty days—I had to be realistic. (Don't ever give yourself spiritual challenges that are impossible to meet.) I'd give it up for several hours a day. That's all. I'd put it in a drawer or a secret pocket of my briefcase where I wouldn't respond to it. Couldn't look at it or look for it for, say, four or five hours.

I failed. Miserably. What if there was an urgent text that I missed? What if my wife was trying to get ahold of me? What if my siblings wanted to contact me with important news about our mom? What if my Instagram friends wondered where I was and what a loser or lousy friend I was by not noticing and liking their cute photos of kids and hikes and birthdays and milestone dinners? What if I fell right off the map?

It's easy enough to say, "Get off social media." But I'm a writer and an editor. I'm a dad, a spouse, and a son. Social media is a way I keep up with the kids and the family. I knew exactly how my then-ninety-year-old mom felt when everybody in the family was talking about cute photos they'd all seen on Facebook or Instagram of someone's birthday party or trip in the Rockies. She wanted to see them too. Her eldest grandson set her up on Facebook, where she friends only family. (Don't you love how *friends* has become a verb?)

I can't be completely out of the know. Our elder son, Will, and his wife live thousands of miles away. They're good about calling regularly—we're lucky they want to hear from us—but in between calls, their posts tell us lots. At least they give us context when we talk to them. "That party looked like it was a lot of fun." "How was the ski trip?" "The new dog is so cute." "Was that a new bike you have?" "Where were you hiking on Saturday?" In the middle of dinner, my wife will get a buzz on her Apple Watch and we'll drop everything to take that call.

I can't get rid of my phone—or my wife her watch—but I can get rid of it controlling me. "Who's in charge here?" I ask it. "You're my phone. I'm not your employee. I'm not required to answer to your every beck and call. Let's work this out."

If meditation is good for anything, it is good for reestablishing the right relationship with material things, like our phones or watches.

Here's the Jesus analogy that comes to mind (one of the weirdest Jesus stories in the Bible): Jesus was with his disciples and noticed the fig tree that had no fruit. He didn't just wag his finger at it and tell his followers, "Hey, you don't want to be unproductive like this." He killed the tree in one fell swoop. Destroyed it.

We're meant to get rid of what doesn't produce fruit in ourselves. Don't coddle our failures of goodness and generosity and abundance; don't make excuses for them; don't work around them. Confront them. Weed out the adversaries. Kill the fig-less tree. I had to do that with my phone. I had to make it my ally in faith, not my enemy. Make more use of the "do not disturb" function. Designate "favorites" and pay attention to that. Why have something in your life that doesn't produce fruit?

Will works in Silicon Valley, the heart of our nation's tech industry. A couple of years back, he and his pals realized how dangerously distracting their cell phones could be, so they established a rule. When they got together for dinner, they put all phones in the center of the table. They'd take them out of their pockets and leave them in a place where they couldn't secretly—or not-so-secretly—check them without everybody noticing. Face-to-face conversation was so much more valuable than anything phoned in. If you have to check that email or text, get up from the table to do it, because it's going to take you out of the room anyway.

Do you find phones have changed habits in other places of your life? At Wednesday night choir rehearsals, we used to get up and chat with one another during our ten-minute break. Now we're more likely to check our phones and catch up remotely. Somehow we feel we have to see what we might have missed in cyberspace during that first hour of rehearsal.

I ignore my phone when I'm meditating. Any message can wait a few minutes. I might look at it when I'm writing at work, but not for long. The writing, the fruit I'm trying to grow or pick, takes precedence. I'm careful about who I follow on social media. Some of it is fruitful to my spiritual life, some is not. Get rid of that fig-less tree.

I follow a couple of art historians on Instagram. They help me see, help me expand my visual vocabulary. Recently one of them pointed out something about Old Master paintings that I'd always been aware of but had never seen explained. In the

Renaissance and the Middle Ages, artists would often depict Jesus and Mary and the disciples in contemporary dress or in contemporary settings. You see David sitting on a throne you could find in the nearest castle, the view out the windows of rolling Tuscan farmland or Mary doing needlework. It's not because the artists had no historical sense. Instead, it was their way of saying, *Jesus is here now.* The disciples are people like us. They could live in houses like ours, dress like us, do the same kind of work that we do. Joseph is a carpenter just like the guy down the block.

That was a welcome insight in the middle of a busy day.

Social media is great. Our phones are great. But watch out.

When I was a kid, Mom would make us have quiet time in our bedrooms. We might have grown out of the nap habit—does anyone completely grow out of that?—but we were still expected to entertain ourselves, use our imaginations for half an hour a day after lunch. We could have a book to read or some toys to play with, but we had to be quiet. I'm sure she did it because she needed a break from us four kids. We were a lot to handle. She needed her quiet time too. But it was also to teach us how to be by ourselves.

If I have taken to zoning out in meditation, it might be thanks to my mom. She prepared me for the experience of being alone in my head. That's hard to do with a phone in your hand. Take notifications. Every buzz or beep comes with the same urgency. Maybe I get two buzzes for texts and just one for email, but they make no distinction between "Could you please pick up some salad stuff on your way home?" and "Call your mom as soon as possible. Something's up."

When we're already overloaded with stress, it can be hard to distinguish between what is urgent, semi-urgent, and not urgent at all. Same thing with that buzz of the phone. Not till I check the text or email will I know.

This is painfully obvious, but if you haven't done it already, figure out what you want to be alerted to and what you'll look for in your own good time. True confession: I don't have my work email linked to my phone. I can easily check in remotely, but I'd prefer to do it on my own schedule. If there's something urgent, my colleagues have my number. At night I have all notifications silenced—except for family emergencies—between 10:00 p.m. and 7:00 a.m. Bless the cell phone. It can set our minds at rest in all sorts of situations. And it can just as easily add to our worries.

Tim was in a high school play the spring of his senior year. We'd given him permission to go to the cast party afterward. At some ungodly hour—11:30 or midnight (I say it's ungodly because those first few hours of sleep always feel the most precious)—the landline rang. I jumped to get it. Too late. There was no answer on the other end and no caller ID. I figured it was Tim and called his cell phone. No answer. Frightening scenarios flashed through my head. He'd been kidnapped. He was in the trunk of some car. He'd tried to call us the one chance he could get—and we missed the call.

I got out the school directory and scanned through it, looking for the phone numbers of his friends. I started dialing. At last, I got through to Nick or Sky or Leo. "This is Tim's dad," I said. "Is Tim there?"

"Well . . . yeah . . . he's right here."

I could hear the noise of the subway. They must have been on that part of the train line that's above ground—you can't get reception below ground between stations. "Tim, it's your dad," the friend said.

"You okay?" I asked.

Bewilderment in his voice: "Yeah, Dad," he said. "We're going to Sky's house."

"Thanks for letting me know." No dead body in the trunk of a car. No disaster. Just an overactive imagination—and a phone.

In the middle of working on this chapter, I had the oddest dream. Carol and I were staying at someone's house on one of those islands off of Cape Cod (Martha's Vineyard or Nantucket or someplace like that), although the name of the town, Tarrytown or Tannersville, had a distinctly Upstate New York ring. We were graced by the visit of one of the original Tanners or Tarrys, a woman dressed in a ball gown. I wanted to show her a picture of a raccoon I'd taken on my phone. He was standing on his hind feet and mimicking me as I'd photographed him, almost as if he were taking a picture of me.

I couldn't find my phone. I checked all the electrical outlets and the cords. Where had I put it? Where had I left it? Carol couldn't find it anywhere either. I thought of a sermon I'd heard about how God speaks to us through both love and suffering. Now I found myself truly experiencing suffering. No phone equaled suffering. The word in the dream to describe this state was *crucifixion.*

If you're like me when someone describes a dream, you probably stopped reading at the second sentence. What surprised me was how crucial to my persona my phone was, a part of my body that I couldn't do without, like my right arm. Jesus told his followers that if your right eye causes you to sin, you should tear it out, or if your right hand causes you to sin, you should cut it off. Better to miss half your body than have your whole body go to hell.

Are we all supposed to be half-blind and missing a hand to be good followers of Jesus? Of course not. But we darn well better pay attention to what gets us in trouble and regulate it or do without it.

Will I give up my phone? No. I have to have it; we don't have a landline anymore. I can't communicate without it. But I don't take its power over me lightly. It's so easy to think of its influence as benign. I don't think it is. Like my right eye and my right hand, it helps me live my life. I can't do without them. I can't do without it. All the more reason to meditate and keep it in its rightful place. Sitting on the sofa next to me, ignored for the time being.

There is the old story of two monks crossing a river. One of them helps a beautiful woman across, carrying her on his shoulders safely to the other side. The other monk is appalled. How could his brother have done such a thing? It went against all their rules, all their spiritual promises. She was beautiful, half-naked. The two of them touched, skin to skin. He'd seen the whole thing. It was monstrous.

At the end of the day he accosted his fellow monk. "How could you? You touched that woman. You held her. What a terrible sin."

"I left that woman back at the river," his brother said. "But you have been carrying her ever since."

Use your phone in such a way that you can forget it. You can live with it and live without it at the same time. I almost got run over by a car in a parking lot the other day because I was star-ing at my phone, consuming some must-read, too-hot-to-handle, latest news story. It couldn't wait. I *had* to read it right then and there. The guy was honking his horn at me, yelling out the window, for good reason. What an embarrassment. What humiliation. As Jesus said, anyone who seeks his life will lose it and anyone who loses his life for Jesus' sake will find it. With or without your phone.

Meditative Moment
Give up the phone for a little while.

Your phone is your friend. But the thing about friends is you choose your time to be with them. You run to their aid. You sit by their hospital bedside. You call them. You send them an encouraging text. You pray for them. And you fiercely guard their privacy, as they do yours.

You have all the cards in this friendship. That friend of a phone wants to do whatever is best for you, as long as you let it. Try this: put your phone aside for ten minutes when you meditate. Turn it off or leave it in another room.

☩☩☩

How'd that go? Not bad, I'll bet. At least you discovered that the world went on without your having to be aware of every niggling news update.

Now, try it for longer. Not just during your prayer time but other times as well. While you're reading a book, while you're eating breakfast, while you're talking to a loved one. Stay out of touch so you can get in touch with something bigger, deeper. Do it for half an hour. An hour. An evening.

†·†·†

Wasn't that nice? It's a gift to your soul.

I don't want to downplay the ways my phone helps me in my spiritual life. Before I meditate, I'm likely to look to the Bible app on my phone for a verse to focus on, a phrase from the Psalms. On a run I'll listen to something spiritual. First thing in the morning I write down whatever dream I can recall, even if it's just a fragment. I won't remember that dream later, but it's there in my phone. Taken together, they form a valuable log of what my dreams are telling me. Not for nothing were dreams considered important in biblical times. They still are.

One last idea: go without your phone for twenty-four hours. Could you possibly do it for a week? Think of it as a sort of silent retreat. See how you miss it. And see how you can use it wisely in your prayer life.

chapter ten

Hold a Good Thought for Others

P ray for others. After all, isn't that what Jesus did?

> As you sent me into the world, so I have sent them into the
> world. I made myself holy on their behalf so that they also
> would be made holy in the truth. I'm not praying only for
> them but also for those who believe in me because of their
> word. I pray they will be one, Father, just as you are in me
> and I am in you. (John 17:18–21 CEB)

I have given myself reminders over the years to pray
for others. I have written names down on Post-it Notes. I
have changed various passwords so that they would be the
names of people or needs I wanted to hold in prayer. I have
worn bracelets made by people who have asked me for their
prayers.

I remember my wife, Carol, once wearing a handcrafted
bracelet a dear friend had made as part of her rehab program
in the hospital. It was there on Carol's wrist for a long while.

Then one day it was gone.

"What happened to that bracelet?" I asked.

"I don't need to wear it anymore."

"Why not?"

"I've got something better. A friend who's well." The prayer
was answered. The reminder was gone.

I don't use reminders as much anymore. No Post-it Notes or

names scrawled in ink on my hand. Instead, I depend on what my mind is telling me.

I sit on the sofa and close my eyes, and even as I release my worries, needs make themselves known. I think of the friend who had open-heart surgery a week ago and has just gotten home from the hospital. Or the dad who is desperately seeking a summer job for his son. Or the recovering alcoholic who has relapsed. Or the writer friend who is dismayed by the pile of rejection letters (it could be me). Or the family facing multiple threats of eviction. Or the woman from the soup kitchen who is sinking into paranoid fantasies.

One measure of a life could be what needs pop into your head when you've given your head a rest. Make them things that count.

Early in my marriage I remember going out to my mother-in-law's place in Connecticut on summer days. All that a person could want seemed to be in rich supply: good food in the refrigerator, fine bottles of wine, a swimming pool waiting for the urban refugee to dive in, a hammock for dozing. All the while I'd listen to her prattle on about what was wrong with the world: the gardener hadn't mowed the herbaceous border, someone she hardly knew had just sent her the ugliest invitation to a wedding shower, the corner gift shop was closing for two weeks, the dry cleaner wasn't making pickups and drop-offs anymore. Rumor had it that the owner of the lot next door was going to build an ugly monstrosity of a house. The world was going to hell in a handbasket.

I made a note to self: if it is the mind's propensity to worry, pick up big worries to put in the mind. Worry about the poor. Worry about those suffering from medical disasters. Worry about the mentally ill. Worry about how you can make a difference in the world. Worry about the least of these.

Go a step further. "Cast all your anxiety on him because he cares for you" (1 Peter 5:7 NIV).

It is tragic to see a homeless couple huddled under a cardboard box in front of an empty storefront or to walk by a scruffy Vietnam vet, dozing in front of a sign asking for donations in an empty cup. Those sights offer pungent reminders of the difficulties to be found in the world and causes to address in a multitude of prayers. Suburban escape offers welcome repose, but I've never wanted it to put me in an insulated bubble. The things that bug us are things that we will want to do something about. Volunteering at our church's soup kitchen is as much a prayer as that dedicated prayer time on the couch. I need them both.

Praying for others is a way of doing something about your worries. You're preventing them from tangling you up in a web of anxiety or putting you in a guilt-ridden role of "angel of mercy." For all the good we want to do, we're bound to get it wrong sometimes. I might have a million plans to sober up that loved one who relapsed—again—but who am I? Do I really know how to help? How will the little that I do or that our church does make a dent in the housing problem?

"Pray as though everything depended on God. Work as though everything depended on you," as the saying goes.

A couple of years ago I landed in the ICU with a mysterious lung infection that stumped all the specialists at NewYork-Presbyterian Hospital. Emails flooded our in-boxes with suggestions on just what treatments the doctors should try or diseases they should test me for. (My wife read the emails, because at that point I was too out of it to read anything.) People wanted to help, and Dr. Google offered myriad suggestions, a rabbit hole to any rescue team. But what did well-meaning friends know that the docs didn't? Was their wisdom so much wiser?

It is human nature to want to fix things, but not everything can be easily fixed. Not for nothing does my primary care provider have a sign up in his office that reads like this: "Patient will be charged extra for any self-diagnosis gotten off the internet."

To pray for something is to give it up, to let it go. To say that we don't really know. (That I was restored to good health I would credit to both the docs and the prayers.)

In the Bible there is the poignant story of David fasting and praying for his first son by Bathsheba. David sprawled on the ground and didn't eat any food, pleading with God for the life of his very ill child. On the seventh day, when the boy died, the servants didn't want to tell him the bad news. *Goodness knows what the man will do.* When he saw them whispering, he guessed at the truth. "Is the child dead?" he asked (2 Samuel 12:19). "Yes," they said.

Then he did the unexpected. He got up, anointed himself with oil, changed out of his dirty clothes, worshipped the Lord, and ate heartily. The servants were mystified. He explained himself, "While the child was still alive, I fasted and wept, for I said, 'Who knows whether the LORD will be gracious to me, that the child may live?' But now he is dead. Why should I fast? Can I bring him back again? I shall go to him, but he will not return to me" (vv. 22–23).

We pray for things in the knowing and not knowing. We

think we have the diagnosis and turn to it to fill the sacred hour. We can be emotionally spent and importunate like David, believing—as we must believe—that our prayers will be answered as we know best. Can we also be like David and accept that we don't know the truth and don't have all the answers? There are times of fasting and times of mourning, and times when we eat again and celebrate, even as we acknowledge our mortality and painful losses. As you may remember, the next thing David did is lie with Bathsheba again and father their second child, Solomon—the font of wisdom, King Solomon.

It is for this reason that I urge you to pray knowing and not knowing. Don't let your fix-it instincts fill the sacred space. Hear your mind offer its prescriptions; acknowledge the depth of your feelings. Then give them up. When someone asks me to pray for them, I'm being asked both to think of them and then not think of them.

My father used the phrase "I'll hold a good thought for you." It was his way of saying, "I'm praying for you." No reason to hold back. Go the whole hog. Even if the doctors have given the patient terrible odds, fill yourself with hope. What do the doctors know? Be like David. See the cure.

What you'll find, as you hold on to that good thought, is that you will also have to let it go. Give it up to a power greater than yourself. That is the process of meditative prayer.

As I've said, I don't use my prayer time to generate brainstorms. All those good ideas can wait—if indeed they're even good ideas. That plot twist in a novel, the great angle for an article I'm writing, that thing I wanted to say in a book about prayer—indeed a book like this—all that can wait. No need to get up and scribble it down. No need to play secretary to my own inspired thoughts. If the idea is any good, it will be there fifteen minutes, twenty minutes, a day later. Similarly with, "I should tell Alex that great idea I have for his son. I can text him right now."

No, not now. I'm doing something much more important.

I'm calling on heavenly powers to make this world a better place. It's not something I can do alone. It might not necessarily be something that God wants to do alone. Many times God chooses to work through us, whether we acknowledge God's power or not. How lovely when people give divine credit for their achievements—that's graciousness itself—but indeed it seems to me that God can also work anonymously, no credit needed. It's inspiration for all of us to do our good works in secret. Thank you, God, for *everything*.

I was recently gorging on the writings of seventeenth-century English mystic Thomas Traherne (1636/37–1674). You can be forgiven if you've never heard of him. I hadn't either until a colleague recently recommended him. In fact, he was little more than a footnote to English literature, an obscure Anglican priest and metaphysical poet. In the late nineteenth century the handwritten folio of his *Centuries of Meditations* was found by a bibliophile in a London bookstall. After much editorial detective work, authorship was finally assigned to Traherne. He'd published a few poems in his short lifetime and rarely put his name to anything (my kind of guy). Some two hundred years later he was discovered.

One of the powerful points he makes is how God is at work through us and in us. "When you love [humans]," he wrote in *Centuries,* the world quickly becometh yours: and yourself become a greater treasure than the world is. For all their persons are your treasures, and all the things in Heaven and Earth that serve them, are yours. For those are the riches of Love, which minister to its Object. You are as prone to love, as the sun is to shine; it being the most delightful and natural employment of the Soul of Man: without which you are dark and miserable.[1]

I keep wanting to stop typing because the thoughts are dense and impenetrable. But Traherne is filled with a felicity—one of his favorite words. Mystics can make you smile and scratch your head at the same time. *You are as prone to love, as the sun is to shine.* Hold on to that thought. To pray for others is to become that loving person you were always meant to be, the mirror of your true self.

Have you ever been on the other side of a one-way mirror and watched people stare at themselves? Or even seen them catch themselves in a glass window as they walk by? You can see them look at themselves and consider what they see. The posture changes; fingers tug at a loose strand of hair; they blink, raise their eyebrows, frown, smile. But when they're looking at themselves, they look least like themselves. Self-consciousness, self-appraisal, self-criticism, self-approval rob them of their naturalness. As soon as they leave the mirror's unforgiving gaze, that loose strand of hair falls back over the forehead, the brow furrows, the slouch returns, but so does that dreamy look in the eye and that impenetrable half smile.

On the other hand, artists' self-portraits can be their best work. Because after looking at themselves in a mirror, they have to see themselves on a canvas, revealing what the mirror can't show: their insides. I'm not so sure about selfies. They tell only a carefully curated truth. I once posted a series of selfies of me singing a song a day for sixty days. As happy as they made me, I was recording them as I was battling depression. Who is that man behind those songs and smiles?

"And as in many mirrors we are so many other selves," Traherne said (writing long before selfies), "so are we spiritually multiplied when we meet ourselves more sweetly, and live again in other persons."[2] *Spiritually multiplied when we meet ourselves in others.* Isn't that a lovely notion?

When William Booth, cofounder of the Salvation Army, couldn't attend the annual Army convention late in his productive life, he was encouraged to send a telegram to the meeting. Because telegrams were expensive and you paid by the word, he decided to meet the challenge by delivering a message that was only one word long (in contrast to his sermons and talks, which could go on). "Others," he wrote.[3] One word said it all.

To give ourselves to others, to be awake to their desires and needs, is to expand our compassionate index. When I look at the photos in my Instagram feed, I feel like I'm stepping into the pleasures of loved ones and family. A selfie that is shared isn't just about the self. It becomes a telegram. Alas, people rarely record their travails in social media. When they do, though, they immediately discover an outpouring of love and concern. The job search, the cancer diagnosis, the death in the family, the unexpected hospitalization: they all become occasions for compassion, and compassion alone can be a prayer for others.

More Traherne: "Of all our desires the strongest is to be good to others. We delight in receiving, more in giving."[4] Or again, "Love is the true means by which the world is enjoyed: Our love to others, and others' love to us."[5]

In the Sermon on the Mount, Jesus said:

You are the light of the world. A city built on a hill cannot be hid. No one after lighting a lamp puts it under the bushel basket, but on the lampstand, and it gives light to all in the house. In the same way, let your light shine before others, so that they may see your good works and give glory to your Father in heaven. (Matthew 5:14–16 NRSV)

Light illuminates; light shows us ourselves. You can see the very words on this page because of light. Your light helps me see myself, and my light might help you shine. We are not mini Statues of Liberty, holding up our lamps. We are the light itself. *You are the light of the world.*

One of my favorite songs to sing at the soup kitchen, and one I always do to encourage some of the younger guests to join in, is "This little light of mine, I'm going to let it shine." It gets more rollicking to add the verse that goes, "Ain't nobody going to blow it out, I'm going to let it shine."[6]

We were all meant to shine, to be the light of the world. But don't lose that part about letting it shine before others, letting them see by our illumination; doing our good works, not just bragging about our inherent brilliance.

This is what comes to me when I pray for others: light. I don't think it's necessary to picture elaborate scenarios of how they might be helped and how our prayers for them should be answered. Like I say, I might not be fully aware of just how they need to be helped. We've all been in situations—or know of situations—where the dark storm cloud turned out to have a silver lining. What I think we're asked to do is feel for someone. Feel their pain, feel their sorrow, feel their joy, feel their happiness. As Traherne put it, "For all their persons are your treasures, and all the things in Heaven and Earth that serve them, are yours. For those are the riches of Love."[7]

When I sink into meditative prayer, people and problems pop up in my mind like actors on the screen. It's always possible, say, to mentally google their names and meander down a byway of accumulated facts and worries, but the whole reason to do this meditative time is to give up those accumulated worries. Why would I add any more to the inventory? Better just to stay with the moment, see the actor on the screen, take in the personage, feel the backstory, then move on. Or at least leave that personage with the screenwriter and director. Don't manipulate it any more than you would a first-rate movie.

Teresa of Ávila made a distinction between verbal prayer and mental prayer.[8] This is the latter. Verbal prayer is when you go through and say all the names of those people you pray for. It doesn't take long. It's worthy and helpful. The one time we regularly do this in our household is grace at dinnertime. We pray out loud for those we're concerned about.

Mental prayer is the silent time. At least, our mouths are silent; the mind is less so. The winningly frank Teresa explained how it took her a much longer time to be able to do mental prayer than verbal prayer. Words came so much easier—and you don't doubt it when you read her. But why limit our options? Why close ourselves off to what we can do without words? Anybody who has written anything knows how limiting words can be. You can only say so much. (That should be painfully obvious to anyone who has stuck with me this far.) Ever needed comfort and discovered how a hug can say so much more than any words? Go for the hug. Give it, receive it, be it, meditate it.

One more quote from Traherne:

How happy we are that we may live in all, as well as one; and how all-sufficient Love is, we may see by this: The more we live in all, the more we live in one. For while He seeth us to live in all, we are a more great and glorious object unto Him; the more we are beloved of all, the more we are admired by Him; the more we are the joy of all, the more blessed we are to Him.[9]

Meditative Moment

Pray with scriptural passages.

I mentioned the practice of lectio divina, *praying your way through Scripture. I've heard of some saintly souls who are making their way through the whole book, line by line, verse by verse, spending a joyous lifetime rigorously meditating on the Word. I'm only capable of doing it here and there, picking a few words, lingering on something that calls my attention.*

Now do it with others in mind. Take a line from the Lord's Prayer: "Give us this day our daily bread" (Matthew 6:11). Notice how Jesus put the whole prayer in the first-person plural, not the singular. I think he's reminding us that as we petition God for our needs, we should be open to those of others. Yes, you need your daily bread (those necessities we cannot do without), but as you ask God, there is that "us."

A name will pop into your head. A concern. Stay there. As you linger on just a short verse, more names will come to you, more needs. You're praying the Bible, but you're also enriching your care for others.

Here are a few other verses you might want to try. Even just a fragment of a verse. A little can go a long way.

"Hold fast to what is good" (Romans 12:9).

"In everything by prayer and supplication with thanksgiving let your requests be made known to God" (Philippians 4:6).

"For surely I know the plans I have for you, says the Lord, plans for your welfare and not for harm, to give you a future with hope" (Jeremiah 29:11 NRSV).

There will be times when meditation feels inscrutable, when your thoughts become too insistent or go into aimless flight. You want a firmer guide than what's in your head (or in a book like this). Use Scripture. Take little bits and pieces, turning them into objects of contemplative prayer.

I'm no clinical psychologist, but it seems to me that this practice is a way to move things from your conscious mind into your unconscious mind, from a place where you try to control everything to a place where your mind will speak silently—and persuasively—to you.

chapter eleven

*Accept
What Seems
Impossible
to Accept*

It is the most profound prayer, the hardest in many ways, and sometimes the easiest. *Not my will but yours be done.* That it was as hard for Jesus to say in the garden in his last hours as it is for us to say in the daily grind of our lives and the Lord's Prayer should offer both comfort and warning. For me, it seems to sum up the meditative act of acceptance. Catherine Marshall, the author behind the popular *Christy* novels, described it as the prayer of relinquishment.[1] Like many believers, she could be harder on herself than she was on anyone else, and yet she knew that God's awesome power was found at those times when we give up being in charge, give up being so certain.

"God helps those who help themselves," goes the old saying. Nothing could be further from the truth.

It was Marshall who reminded me, years ago, that in fact God helps those who allow themselves to be helpless, who give up all their brilliant stratagems and plans to honor what a higher power has to offer. One gift the twelve-step movement has offered us—those in recovery and those of us who love people who have had the courage to battle their addictions—is the power of admitting to powerlessness. It's the beginning of everything.

But how on earth do we get there? How do we make our way to sublime relinquishment? When do we stop asking and stop haranguing? It doesn't mean stifling the complaints and giving up the dealmaking. It is only human to badger—even when we're badgering God. But the gift of meditative prayer, as we do it over and over again, is to finally let go of the haranguing. We become so silent in ourselves that we can accept whatever God has in mind—God's joyful surprise.

True confession: it startles me again and again how pig-headed and stubborn I can be, how sure of myself, how confident in my rightness. I think I know everything. I'm not talking about cosmic stuff, like grace and forgiveness and trust and hope, but about mundane issues, like what year the movie *Titanic* came out and who was the president of the United States before McKinley and where I put the checkbook and how much money we have in our account and didn't I tell you at least three times that we're meeting so-and-so at X or Y to discuss W and Z? Doesn't anybody ever listen to me?

Words I can never say too often: "I was wrong. I'm sorry. Please forgive me. I didn't mean to be so arrogant."

Years ago, when I was a kid, I was surprised when Mom and Dad's best friend, Uncle Larry, said something about his relationship to Aunt Martha. They had been married as long as Mom and Dad and seemed to have as solid a relationship as my parents did. So why did Uncle Larry say to me, "Marriage takes a lot of work"? What was he talking about? Work like raking the leaves in the backyard, or going to the office and typing a million memos? Work like practicing the piano for hours so that you could remember the piece you were going to play in that recital and your hands wouldn't fall off the keys?

That love should take work was quite a surprise, and yet it does. Love of others and love of God. Love of self too. Work like sitting and meditating on the couch every morning, praying silently.

Part of the work of marriage is brutal honesty, especially honesty with yourself. Discovering your imperfections even before they are pointed out, doing combat with your expectations, watching out for projections ("How come you're not my mother?"), learning to love over and over. As you need to be present in your relationship with God, you need to be present in your relationships with those you love.

The inner noise, the assertive ego, will pop up all over the place. Better that it pops up in my meditation time and gets addressed than pops out of my mouth in a few barbed words. "Where two or three are gathered in my name," Jesus said, "there am I among them" (Matthew 18:20). I don't think it was just about safety in numbers. Companionship is essential for discipleship—to be a follower of Jesus—not just for collaboration and support but also for correction. "Why did you say that?" we ask. "What did you mean by that? Help me understand."

The apostle Peter made a remarkable transformation in the space of a few pages in the Bible. In the Gospels he was often the overenthusiastic doofus. He stepped out of the boat to follow Jesus, walking on water—and in a sudden loss of trust, almost sank. When Jesus spoke of what was to come, that he would be killed and then raised on the third day, Peter said, "God forbid." His outburst inspired the rebuke from Jesus, "Get behind me, Satan" (Matthew 16:22–23 CEB). So much for the bedrock of faith.

Jump ahead to the book of Acts, and Peter had become a different person. It was as though a new actor walked in the room. He performed miracles. He gave sermons that went on for many verses. He risked his life to preach the Good Word. He discovered his gifts for apostleship. It is as though he had to do it all wrong in the Gospels to get it right in the end.

Where he really lost it, where he seemed to break Jesus' heart, was right before the crucifixion, when he promised that he would stick by Jesus' side—and then he denied that he even knew the Lord, fulfilling Jesus' prediction, "Before the rooster crows, you will deny me three times" (Matthew 26:34; one of several likely reasons that a rooster often crowns a church tower).

If Peter could become a model for prayer, so can we. In fact, I think that's the whole point of the messiness of our faith. It mirrors the messiness of life. We're going to get things wrong, we're going to fall short, so that we can finally get it all right. Those resurrection moments are always right around the corner.

Let's go back to Jesus in the garden. He was going through agony. According to some accounts he was actually sweating blood. Because he is God, he knew what was about to happen. Because he is also human, he had to wallow in the fear of it, the torturous anticipation of terrible pain and total abandonment. "Abba, Father," he prayed, calling God by the most intimate of names, "remove this cup from me" (Mark 14:36). It is what any of us would say: "I can't go through it. I don't want to do it. Take it away." *If you are God, you could fix this. You could make it all disappear. You could change everything in the blink of an eye.* Even if it hasn't happened, the mere prospect is misery.

Then quickly—almost too quickly to take in—Jesus said, "Not what I want but what you want" (v. 36 CEB). There it is: *not my will but thy will be done.* Sublime, divine acceptance. Help for the helpless, power to the powerless, release for the suffering, purpose in purposelessness, truth in emptiness, substance in nothing.

Contemplative, meditative prayer will take you to this place. It's the biggest, most important, most challenging, most rewarding goal of the spiritual life.

Think of it: Jesus, praying in the garden, experiencing the epitome of a sleepless night. His dearest deputy, Peter, who was supposed to watch out, was asleep. Jesus let him have it. (Like a good screenplay, the Bible often puts the best stuff in dialogue. Show, don't tell.) "Simon, are you asleep? Could you not keep awake one hour? Keep awake and pray that you may not come into the time of trial; the spirit indeed is willing, but the flesh is weak" (Mark 14:37–38 NRSV).

Yes, we say, *I want to do this.* Then we fall asleep at the wheel.

Jesus wanted that cup of suffering wrested from him, wrung out of his hands. At the same time, he knew what was up. More than any of us can know, he knew what was ahead. Disaster, torture, death. Still, it didn't prevent him from staying there in the garden, awake, praying. That's the model he was giving to Peter—to stay with the Spirit.

I do the dishes at home. Carol does the cooking. She's a better cook than I am, and I actually enjoy doing the dishes. I like the sound of the water tumbling out of the faucet, the mini waterfall, the feel of it on my hands, the sloshing of sponge and detergent in the sink, the challenge of scrubbing. Doing the dishes is one of those rare tasks in life where you can actually see change. What was dirty is now clean. What was mired in grease and oil now shines.

Every once in a while, there is that pot or pan with grime

and crud on it that doesn't come off with the scrubbing pad and elbow grease, no matter how long you work at it. Carol often has to remind me, "Just let it soak."

You fill up the pot or pan with warm water and just leave it in the sink for a couple of hours. You come back, and bingo, all that stuff that was so impossible to get off floats at the top. A little soap and the thing's like new.

When Jesus prayed, "Not what I want but what you want," he was letting himself soak in the Spirit. Things were at their worst, and he needed all the help he could get.

In the first three Gospels, the Synoptic Gospels, as they're called, we read pretty similar accounts of his misery before the crucifixion, but in the Gospel of John, Jesus is more philosophical as he prepares to meet the end. He seems to step back, having a greater perspective on what is happening. Holy acceptance is given words, silence allowed a soundtrack.

"Father, the time has come." *The time has come.* "Glorify your Son, so that the Son can glorify you. You gave him authority over everyone so that he could give eternal life to everyone you gave him. This is eternal life: to know you, the only true God, and Jesus Christ whom you sent. I have glorified you on earth by finishing the work you gave me to do. Now, Father, glorify me in your presence with the glory I shared with you before the world was created" (John 17:1–5 CEB).

This voice is so different from the one in the other Gospel accounts. No agony, just distilled wisdom. Part of me wonders: How did the writer of the Gospel of John know Jesus prayed these words? Was he a reporter hiding in the bushes or behind a bureau? Was he peeking out of a window? Then I dismiss all that journalistic silliness. The Gospels are not the *New York*

Times. They are windows into our souls. Jesus is praying for his followers. He is praying for *us*.

> They don't belong to this world, just as I don't belong to this world. Make them holy in the truth; your word is truth. As you sent me into the world, so I have sent them into the world. I made myself holy on their behalf so that they also would be made holy in the truth.
>
> I'm not praying only for them but also for those who believe in me because of their word. I pray they will be one, Father, just as you are in me and I am in you.
>
> I pray that they also will be in us, so that the world will believe that you sent me. I've given them the glory that you gave me so that they can be one just as we are one. I'm in them and you are in me so that they will be made perfectly one. (John 17:16–23 CEB)

Heady stuff. Of course, it's doctrine in the guise of narrative, the basis of a thousand sermons, the subject of countless essays, books, and dissertations. But it's also prayer, extraordinary prayer. Words that go beyond words.

Jesus did this. We get to do this.

How?

Here's what I like to do when I meditate: give myself a word or a phrase and spin that around in the silence. *You are in me. God. I am in you. Jesus, Jesus, Jesus.* Sometimes I meditate on the word *way.* After all, the first followers of Christ were often called people of the Way (Acts 9:2). I do *truth*, too, believing that God's presence in me, the Spirit doing the work, can lead me to inner truth. And of course, the word *Spirit*. These are all avenues for acceptance. It is to get to that split-second eternal state of "Thy will be done."

My favorite picture of the ascension is the one at the Met museum, painted in the sixteenth century, showing the disciples all gazing up to the clouds. All they can see, or at least all that is shown in the picture, are Jesus' sandaled feet.[2] Just that glimpse. They are caught in that moment. They've heard those promises; they've seen him on earth; they've witnessed his resurrection. Now what? They're still looking up, waiting. Would that they look within. Won't the Spirit come?

The whole concept of the Holy Spirit was a bit baffling to me as a kid. Father God, that was easy enough to understand. And Jesus, that wasn't hard to figure out. There were those sentimental pictures of Jesus in our Sunday school room. He had a beard and a robe, and at Christmas he was a baby in a manger. But the Holy Spirit, or the Holy Ghost, as it was often called back then? Nobody could give me a picture of that. Nobody could show me what it looked like. "It's like the wind," my Sunday school teacher would say. "We can't see it, but we can feel it and we can observe what it does, the way the wind blows the leaves from the trees." That didn't help much.

Then I flew my first kite. I built it out of balsa wood and paper from a kit we got at the toy store. I had lots of string because I expected it to fly high, over the oak trees and the pear tree in front of our house, rising next to the swaying palms.

The hard part was just trying to get it up in the air. I ran down the block, tugging at the string, feeling the kite rise above me, but when I turned around, it drifted down again, its tail landing on the sidewalk like a snake. My boyhood friend David convinced me that maybe if we tied one end of the kite to my bike, we could make it rise in the air, letting out the string slowly.

The kite went up with me steering the bike and David racing behind. But the kite fell again back to earth. We couldn't make it fly, couldn't get it airborne.

Then one exceptionally clear autumn day when the Santa Ana winds had driven the fog and smog out to sea and the mountains rising above Pasadena were so easy to see that you felt that you could reach out and touch them, we got the kite out from the closet and grabbed hold of it. We stood on the sidewalk on the corner and pushed the kite into the air. It wasn't so windy on the ground, but you could see from the way the tall royal palms were leaning that the wind was blowing hard. The breeze caught our kite like magic, lifting it from where David was holding it, sending it flying. The tail made out of torn sheets danced above his head.

We let out the string and the kite rose higher and higher. We were very careful to keep it away from any kite-mauling palms; previous victims could be seen on the swaying trunks. We tugged on the string, straddling the sidewalk and the street. Soon it was so small, dancing in the air, that I figured it would rise above an airplane or jet, getting close to a faded sliver of moon. Were it not for the string, the kite would rise straight to the sun.

All it took was time, patience, trust, persistence. We kept putting ourselves in the right place, holding on to the string.

And then one day it flew. Like that power we can't see that will lift us up and carry us in ways we couldn't possibly imagine.

Meditative Moment

Hum a prayer.

You might not want to do this where anyone can hear you. It says something, for sure, how loud city life is that no one seems to overhear me if I'm humming to myself, "God, God, God" on the subway. Or it says something about the boundaries of urban life, that if you notice some dude on the subway humming with his eyes closed—and he doesn't even have any headphones on—you do all you can to avoid him and, if possible, move away.

It's easiest to do this with your mouth closed and your lips sealed. The holy word you've picked, whether it's God or love or Jesus, is not something you're going to sing out loud, but it's a word or phrase you hold in your head while you hum.

Pick a note that goes with the natural resonance of your body. Rap your knuckles on a piece of wood, ping a half-full glass of water with a spoon; they will resonate to a certain note. Play a set of scales on a musical instrument and notice how a vase on a table will vibrate to one note. I find if I hum through a series of notes, I can feel how they resonate in my body. The sweet spot is somewhere an octave below middle C. That's where I get the deepest inner vibration.

(I suspect that people who have perfect pitch have this same sense of themselves. They can

tell what note they're hearing by the way it feels. They're in tune with their bodies.)

Don't get too wrapped up in what note it is or why it feels good to you. Just try out different notes and see how they feel. There might be a couple you want to use. Close your eyes and hum. Breathe in silently; hum as you release the breath. Hold your sacred word in your head as you hum. Breathe again. Keep at it. Do it for a minute.

⁑·⁑

I call it holy humming, a chance to reconnect with eternity. As the old saying goes, "The one who sings prays twice." Why not humming too?

chapter twelve

Praise God from Whom All Blessings Flow

E ven silence is praise. The end of all things and the beginning. I have often wondered why God would need or want praise. Is God really that insecure? Is God like a boss who expects his underlings to fawn all over him? Are we supposed to tell God, "You're wonderful, you're fabulous, you're the great strong and mighty" to shore up God's fragile ego? Why sing all those songs of praise? Why thank God in dozens of psalms? There's got to be a reason.

I've seen how important praise is in the workplace. You can never thank and praise your employees and colleagues enough. We so often point out things that are under par, achievements that might have missed the boat, places where there is room for improvement, and forget to point out what is right. Some people will protest, "Why should I thank somebody just for doing their job? That's what they're supposed to do. Why praise them?"

Because we're all much more likely to go that extra mile when we feel valued and recognized. We light up, our energies recharged.

People need to know they're hitting the mark. They need to see how they're measuring up. Don't wait for the annual review. Or with family and friends, don't wait for some milestone birthday. Thank them now. Remind them how much they mean to you. Give credit where credit is deserved. What a gift for them.

I seem to have two tapes playing inside my head at the same

time, one that says, *Gosh, I'm pretty good, aren't I?* and the other one that says, *Boy, what a disaster I made of that.* All the more important for me to hear that I did something right—if I can receive the compliment. (My wife and I have had more than one discussion on how to receive praise because I'm not always good at it. "Just say thanks," she says. "Don't tell me how unjustified my praise might be.")

I would also argue that we praise people for *us*, for the benefits *we* derive from it. When I praise a coworker or a friend, it's a chance to acknowledge to myself as well as to them that their work or friendship makes a difference. That I couldn't do what I do without them. That their insights, their smarts, their wisdom, open up my world. They help me see things that I wouldn't normally see. Even their criticism (as hard as it might be to take in) has had an impact on me. Often at work I have felt like I'm playing tennis with people who are just a notch or two better than me—or several notches. When someone else is at the top of their game, they make your game look great. Praise is my chance to own that.

What then about praising God?

I like to picture God up there—or down here—saying, "I don't need you to tell me how great I am. I know that already. Didn't I create the universe? Didn't I create you in my own image? The world is an awe-inspiring masterpiece. Go ahead and praise me for it. Savor it with every sunset. Here's what I want you to think about: every time you sing my praises, you look just a little bit more like me. It's not for me; it's for *you.*"

Being generous and grateful is Godlike. Looking for the best, seeing the best in others, recognizing their soulful properties and saying something about it. People who praise people and praise God are praiseworthy. They are humble in the best sense of the word.

Ever been complimented for something you didn't think was noticeable or even worthy? That person is giving you a bit more of yourself while doing themselves a favor. You become bigger when you see how big someone else is, how precious, how glorious and lovable in God's sight. Give it back to the Creator. Celebrate God's goodness. Make it a party; invite others; the more the merrier.

Remember the parable of the lost sheep? The man has one hundred sheep—which is a lot of sheep—and he loses one of them. He searches high and low until he finds the one and then celebrates. He calls all his friends and neighbors together and they have a party. "Celebrate with me because I've found my lost sheep" (Luke 15:6 CEB). When the parable is talked about, we usually emphasize the one-in-a-hundred aspect. Everyone counts. Nothing is right until we're all found. The lost one matters as much as the ninety-nine. But don't forget the celebration. It's a big deal. The guy calls all his friends and neighbors and probably uncorks his best bottle of wine or grills the fatted calf. He surely spent more on the party than he would have replacing the one lost sheep. Celebration matters, rejoicing in the recovered soul.

Or take the parable of the woman who has ten silver coins and loses one of them. She lights a lamp and sweeps the house to find it, looking high and low. When she finally does uncover it, she reaches out to her friends and neighbors, saying, "Celebrate with me because I've found my lost coin" (v. 9 CEB). Once again, the party could easily cost more than the single lost coin—and this lady only has ten coins, so her means are modest—but celebration is all-important. Jesus said, "I tell you, joy breaks out in the presence of God's angels over one sinner who changes both heart and life" (v. 10 CEB). If God's angels can celebrate over our right choices, our turning from the wrong ones, gosh, shouldn't we?

How on earth did Christianity get its reputation for being dour? How did we miss all these signs of joy?

When I'm really out of sorts, when I'm plummeting into a pit, when I only want to sing the blues, I have taken to actually writing down the things I'm grateful for. I make a list. It sounds so dorky, but it is necessary and essential. Write them down. Hold them in your head and heart. Because it's so easy to lose touch with all the good reasons for praise. It's like being disconnected from those angels who break out in joy.

The thing about praise is that we think of it as noisy, raucous. We think of making that joyful noise the psalmist talks about. Imagine, though, how you can do it in silence.

When I was a kid and couldn't sleep, my dad would come and sit on the side of my bed, rubbing my back for a minute. Then he'd talk me through the different parts of my body from my foot to my head, talking me to sleep. It was like a guided meditation before I even knew there were such things. "Feel your toes falling asleep. See how relaxed they are? They're falling asleep, one by one. Now your legs are relaxing; they're so tired they're sleeping too . . ."

I would never fall asleep right away, but a smile would come across my face. My father was letting me know I was loved. He was there with me. I could sing his praise. Not a word was spoken on my part—after all, I was supposed to be falling asleep—but I bubbled up with gratitude from within. Silent praise.

Another comparison that comes to mind is what happens with a really good performance of a play or a concert or even after a sermon. A silence comes over an audience or congregation that's profound. As a performer, I've been lucky enough to feel it just a few times, that sense that you're with a group of people and they're with you, and if you could hold on to that silence for a moment longer, you would be able to rule the world. It's bigger than all of you put together. The silence is holy. It's the greatest compliment you could possibly give to a performer, appreciative silence. You don't want to clap because you don't want to break the spell.

I can imagine God loving silence like that just like any of us do. Maybe loving it because it's a shared silence. God is in it with us.

When you enter into contemplative prayer, all sorts of negative emotions will come up. We've talked about that. You need to pay attention to them. Don't think that the more you do prayer like this, the quieter the emotions will become. Not at all. What happens, though, is you get a little more used to listening to those emotions and recognizing them, putting them in their rightful place. Jealousy, anger, greed, self-pity, self-righteousness, and small-mindedness can take a back seat. You can replace them with praise, gratitude, love, hope, faith, and silence. Long-term companions.

Contemplative prayer is a process. You may be perfect at it; I'm not. And that is a source of pleasure. I get to work at it; I get to dip into silence; I get to make a place for it, seat it at the table. I get to praise God with my mouth shut and my eyes closed and my body still. The urge sometimes comes to raise a hand. Want to pray sitting at your desk? Raise a hand. Raise both hands.

Your colleagues will think you're simply stretching. You're doing that too. But you're also reaching for the heavens. They're not so far away. Right there above your desk and at your feet, all around you. Imagine that.

It's no surprise to me that "How Great Thou Art" is one of the most popular hymns. God's greatness is ours to share. Reflected glory. "Then sings my soul, my Savior God to thee," go the lyrics. "How great thou art, how great thou art."[1] It's my soul that sings. Yours too.

"Since God cannot be imagined, anything our imagination tells us about Him is ultimately misleading and therefore we cannot know Him as He really is unless we pass beyond everything that can be imagined and enter into an obscurity without images and without the likeness of any created thing," Thomas Merton wrote in his book *New Seeds of Contemplation*.[2]

I used to think, *Gosh, it would have been easy for a Trappist like Merton to meditate. After all, he was in a spiritual community. He was a monk living a cloistered life. Everybody around him was praying.* But reading Merton, I'm often reminded that challenges for Trappist monks are the same that we face in the world. The distractions are just as intense, if not more so. The mental discipline is just as demanding. No need to make excuses where you are, where I am, wherever we are. The narrow gate is right there around the corner for us to enter.

If I can't depend on my imagination, what can I depend on? Silence. This place dedicated to silence. This moment of looking to the cloud of unknowing. Unknowing is so counterintuitive. I spend far more time doing just the opposite. Knowing. Acquiring knowledge. Showing off my smarts. Disagreeing with others, pointing out what I know. Secure in what I've learned. In too many discussions I'm all too ready to point out some little-known fact that I happen to have at my fingertips. I was once a contestant on a TV game show, *Tic-Tac-Dough*, and won a free trip to Europe for two and a dining room set, not to mention $1,500, because I knew stuff. I could come up with the right answers and was rewarded for them. How completely counter-cultural to establish a practice of *not* knowing. (The question I couldn't answer was, "Who was Phyllis Diller's husband?" Fang!)

The past century has brought mind-boggling discoveries and scientific breakthroughs. And yet, the wonder of science is in how much more there is to be known. How much we don't know. A psychiatrist friend reminded me the other day, over lunch, just how much we don't know about the brain and how it works. Maybe only about 5 percent is completely understood. Think of how much remains to be discovered! Think of the scientific breakthroughs that are ahead!

One of my friends, a woman of profound spiritual intelligence, tells about a key moment in her development as a believer. A great lover of the outdoors, she was hiking in the wilderness on the back side of the Sierras. She climbed a mountain peak in that dry, desertlike terrain and gazed out over endless acres of wilderness, and her heart was filled. All that she wanted was there. God spoke to her, grabbing her in the nothingness. Although she now lives in bustling, crowded New York City, she still keeps in emotional touch with that place of emptiness. The mountains, the hills, the desert, the sky, a horizon that seems limitless, a view that goes on forever, foreground and background merging together, and wind the only sound.

Should it be any surprise that the place Jesus went to before he could begin his ministry was the desert? It was a place of trial and temptation—and where he found out what he was meant to do.

Be gobsmacked; be amazed; be astonished. "Words can't begin to describe . . ." we say about something that is beyond our understanding. What could be further beyond our understanding than God?

This little book has tried to be about embracing the silence, chasing after it, savoring it, using it, making it a part of your everyday. But there comes a time, too, when you have to get up from the sofa, the cushion, the chair, the bed. When you have to open your eyes and do. You might have just gotten hit with a mystical moment; you might have seen your own version of the angels ascending and descending as they did on Jacob's ladder. You might want to hold on to that forever. Don't. You need to let it go.

I remember teaching my Sunday school kids about the transfiguration. How Jesus took three of his disciples to the top of a mountain, where he was transformed in front of them, his clothes turning whiter and brighter than if they'd been washed with the strongest bleach, and how Elijah and Moses appeared with Jesus, talking to him.

Peter's response was that they should make three tabernacles—or booths, in the translation we used—one for Moses, one for Elijah, and one for Jesus. With my Sunday school kids we tried to imagine how they would do this, constructing something with branches and boughs, maybe a few planks. The kids thought cardboard boxes would do. Peter wanted to hold on to the moment, clinging to it, to hold on to this weird, mystical thing that was happening in front of him. But it couldn't be stopped; it couldn't be frozen in time. A cloud overshadowed them, and a voice spoke from a cloud: "This is my beloved Son: hear him" (Luke 9:35 KJV). Then just as fast as it came, it was gone. The moment was over.

I look to the example of the transfiguration in my prayer time. That should I be visited by any transcendent moments—and goodness, I've never had a vision like that—they are to be observed and celebrated and honored, but there's no prolonging them. No building of tabernacles, no making of shrines. Just a momentary sense of wonder and gratitude. Then a waking up and a moving on. I don't doubt that those glimpses of God's presence, however small and transitory, feed us and nourish us, but there's no holding on to them. We are overcome by wonder—stunned by the wonder. Resist the impulse to intellectualize, to overthink it. Remember how Jesus told the three disciples not to say anything about the transfiguration to anyone just yet (Matthew 17:9). To keep silent.

Because silence is praise? Maybe.

No matter what, whether you've seen visions or not, give yourself a transition moment. Sit there for a while. Take a whole minute or two. Listen to what's going on around you. See it. Then get up and do what you have to do. Log on to the computer; respond to those texts you ignored while sitting. Make that shopping list. Run that errand. Go to that meeting. Send that email.

You might still be asking that question, "How long should I pray? How long should I meditate?" Five minutes that are truly dedicated to silence can be precious. If that's what you've got, go for it.

There was a group that met early in the mornings in our apartment complex one day a week for meditation. I loved the idea and loved the group. But the timing wasn't always right. I find it easier to fit meditation in on my own schedule. Still, I don't doubt there is a divine power in practicing contemplative prayer en masse. "Where two or more are gathered . . ." Just be practical. Do what works. Even if I might be all alone sitting on my sofa, overhearing the dog walkers outside or the school bus lumbering by, I don't feel alone. Others are doing what I'm doing all around the world, at any time of day or night, in every time zone. We are one.

Like I said earlier, I cling to the notion, hopelessly optimistic, profoundly hopeful, that we are changing the world as we change ourselves. Making it a place of peace as we forge inner peace in our beings. We do it. And then we get up and live it. We honor our practice by stepping away from it. It's still there. Every bone in my body remembers it. "The song is ended, but the melody lingers on," as the old Irving Berlin lyric goes.[3]

Music is defined not just by the notes you sing or play but by the silence in between them. Back to what the psalmist said: "Even silence is praise" (Psalm 65:1 CEB). For you, for me, for all of us.

Meditative Moment

Throw your body into it.

I talked about yoga at the beginning of this book. Something it offers that we often lose in Christianity is a physical practice to go with the mental. You move your body in an inner and outer journey of peace.

Even when you're sitting on your sofa or your pillow or your chair, deep into meditative silence, you can do the same. You can give yourself small gestures to echo or encourage what's going on inside.

Lean back and raise your head aloft so your eyes can see the ceiling—or the heavens—if you have your eyes open.

Turn your head slowly to the right, as though you are looking behind you. Turn your head slowly to the left, as though you are looking behind you. Do it with eyes open or eyes closed. You're turning away from the bad, turning toward the good, opening up to God's goodness. Raise a hand or both hands, the way we sometimes raise our hands in church when we're overcome with the Spirit.

Now use tapping fingers to activate the healing power in your body. Key points to tap (meridians, as they're called): above the eyebrows, on the side of your head next to the eyes, beneath the ears, on the chin just below your lips, on your collarbone, on the palms of your hands (where Christ's nails are traditionally pictured as having gone), on your knees.

Say to yourself a sacred word or a short prayer like, "Jesus Christ, have mercy on me, a sinner." Tap lightly but strong enough to feel it in your fingers and wherever you're tapping. Now sit quietly, your hands open in your lap or on your knees.

According to C. S. Lewis, St. Augustine once said, "God wants to give us something, but cannot, because our hands are full—there is nowhere for Him to put it."[4] Well, your hands are now open. You are ready to receive.

Acknowledgments

Big thanks to my colleagues at Guideposts, among them Edward Grinnan, Amy Wong, Colleen Hughes, Hilary Ribons, Ansley Roan, Jim Hinch, Evan Miller, Celeste McCauley, and Kimberly Elkins, who have nurtured me and taught me and put up with me over the years. You are among my beloveds, helping me write and pray at the same time. I'm grateful to my family, especially my immediate family: our boys, Will and Tim, and my wife, Carol. Thanks to my faith community and their incalculable role in my spiritual growth over the years, especially our Tuesday night group—Tom Phillips, thanks for your suggestions on this book. Blessed be my agent, Bob Hostetler, who stuck with me, never giving up hope. Kudos to my editor, Kyle Olund, for his wisdom, faith, knowledge, and good humor. Special callout to Jeanette Levellie for her eagle-eyed insights and kind suggestions upon reading an early draft. And thanks to all who have prayed for me and for whom I pray, especially our church soup-kitchen guests. Godspeed.

Thirty Days of Prayer

M any of us—if not most of us—can find the prospect of meditation daunting. There are so many challenges, not the least of which is our own fear of failure. Fret not. Humility about the process can be your greatest friend. Your own insecurity is fertile ground. All it takes is a seed, that mustard seed. Here are a few ways you can plant those seeds in a day-by-day experience of self-nurture and delight in a thirty-day journey to move forward in faith.

Day 1. Listen. As a kid I used to wonder how those people in the Bible were able to listen to God. How did they do that? Then I'd hear my mom say, "You have to stop talking all the time and listen to me." Be quiet. Get silent. Schedule a time when you will be silent with God, even if it's just a few minutes. Then throughout the day, notice how the silence rings true.

Day 2. Find a place. God can find you anywhere. But it can be easier to pray if you go back to the same place again and again, making it your holy place, even if it's just an old easy chair or a corner of your bedroom. It's your sacred space. Choose it. Bless it with a prayer or two. Then sit there—or lie there—and make it your own. All the external stimuli will be your call to worship.

Day 3: Try a word, one word. It might be something from Scripture. *God, love, mercy, hope, Jesus, sin, forgiveness.* Use it to focus your mind. There's a lot going on in your head. So much noise. Silence has revealed that to you. The word you choose will be a way to bring you back to the heavenly from your worldly concerns and fears. Find the power in a word.

Day 4: Be in comfortable silence. Loved ones can communicate without saying a word, just by being in each other's presence. It's the same for you. God is present, and you're making yourself present for God. There might be a thousand thoughts going through your head, but you don't have to say a thing. The shared silence is a mutual blessing. Think of how much it must mean to God.

Day 5: Notice the distractions. You've been doing this for five days now, and it bothers you how easily distracted you are. Not just the noise outside your window but the stuff that flies through your brain. Hear it; see it; notice it. Then let it go. In prayer. If you resist the distraction, it will only get bigger. If you pay attention to it, you can do something about it. Give it over to God.

Day 6: Turn to a psalm. The Psalms are a rich resource. Too often I find myself simply reading them rather than praying them. Your prayer time is a chance. Take just one line of a psalm and meditate on that. Or make it shorter each time you say it. "Be still and know that I am God." "Be still and know that I am . . ." "Be still and know . . ." Till you get to "Be . . ." with God.

Day 7: Rejoice in your humility. Jesus tells the story of the publican and the Pharisee, the latter full of self-congratulatory prayers, the publican feeling inadequate, asking for God's mercy as he approaches the temple. Whom does Jesus single out? The latter. "Blessed are the poor in spirit," Jesus said (Matthew 5:3). The poor in spirit. That's a place where you are much blessed. Go with it.

Day 8: Breathe a prayer. God gave us humans the breath of life. Using your breath in a prayer is a way to reconnect with that. Breathe in the love of God. Breathe out those negative emotions: fear, anger, frustration, worry. Hold on to the love of God with each breath, then let it go as you let go of those things that get in the way of that love. You can breathe such little prayers all day.

Day 9: Give to others. Let your meditations open you up to the opportunities. A need will pop into your head, a concern, a way to help. A phone call you can make, an email to send, an encouraging word to pass along, a check to write. We express our faith both vertically and horizontally, looking to the heavens and giving to our neighbors. Both are forms of prayer.

Day 10: Let go of the self-criticism. My head can be full of words of self-congratulation and just as full of niggling critiques. Sometimes I wonder if the former is an attempt to make up for the latter. Prayer is an opportunity to reset. If God can forgive me for my failures, why can't I? We are to love our neighbors as ourselves—*as ourselves.* "Forgive me, God," I pray.

Day 11: Praise God. Praise is rich, fulfilling, and good for the soul. It's a chance to give credit and thanks to God for all the good things that have come your way. Come up with five things that you are especially grateful for. Write them down. Hold them in your head. Then praise God. As we used to say at church camp: "Rub-a-dub-dub, thanks for the grub, yeah, God!"

Day 12: Don't look at the clock. You might start worrying about how much time this is taking. You might yearn to open your eyes and check the clock or your phone or your watch. Two ideas: set a timer to keep track of the time so you don't have to, and set your phone on "do not disturb" for that time. You're going into a place beyond time and space (and your watch).

Day 13: Pray through anger. It's perfectly natural to have moments of anger when you pray. Don't run away from them. You might replay some perceived injustice—from yesterday or from long ago. It might still infuriate you. Don't bury it. Notice it. Express your anger, even if it might be addressed to God. God can take it. Then experience God's infinite forgiveness and love.

Day 14: Keep at it. We often call it the practice of prayer—*practice* being the operative word. Sometimes you'll wonder if you're getting anywhere or growing at all. It seems like so much work. Why bother? Remind yourself: trying to do it *is* doing it. In prayer, the trying *is* the doing. You cannot fail. Practice makes perfect because the practice *is* perfect.

Day 15: Let your light shine. "You are the light of the world," Jesus said (Matthew 5:14). Let it shine. The brightest lights in our home are hooked up to electricity. Guess what? That's what you're doing every day: plugging yourself in to the power source. Picture that source. God's light is there, waiting to illuminate you as you linger in prayer. Plug in.

Day 16: Pray without ceasing. The apostle Paul's admonition to "pray without ceasing" can feel intimidating (1 Thessalonians 5:17). How do you pray in the middle of a busy day? Getting into the habit is what gets you there. The words you use, the powerful silence you have given yourself, can be called upon in little bits and bursts throughout a day. God's love is without ceasing.

Day 17: Pray for others. "Hold a good thought" is how my father put it. Holding a good thought is enough. It's more than enough. Your compassion for whatever someone might be going through—a scary surgery, marital troubles, financial losses—is part of that prayer. Your compassion will stay with you long after your prayer time is over. Those good thoughts will be passed along.

Day 18: Change the world. Did you not realize that's what you're doing? We change the world by changing ourselves, by growing. Each day of prayer is a step toward that. Picture all the other people who are doing the same thing as you are. Countless souls. We might not see each other or hear each other, but God hears all of us together.

Day 19: Go for a walk. A prayer walk. Get in touch with the Creator by taking a meditative walk in the creation. Stare at the sky, the clouds, the trees, the grass. Breathe the air. Don't listen to a podcast. Don't make this a time to call a friend. Just walk and feel the wonder of creation. Let yourself be transformed and inspired by that.

Day 20: Acknowledge any pains. You are sitting quietly in a meditative moment—and all at once you can feel that ping in your back, something you've been ignoring for a while. Notice it now. Ask God to be part of your healing. Maybe it's something you need to see a doctor or a physical therapist for. They are collaborators in your healing. With God.

Day 21: Go without words. Can't even find the words to pray? Not even sure what to put before God? As Paul reminded us, "The Spirit himself intercedes for us with groanings too deep for words" (Romans 8:26). Being wordless is a powerful place to be when you let the Holy Spirit do the work. That's what prayer is: letting God take charge.

Day 22: Notice the noise. Every morning when I sit on the sofa, trying to get quiet, I can hear all sorts of noises. Birds chirping, cars going past, a dog barking, a distant siren. We talked about how distractions can only get bigger if you ignore them. It's the same with those noises. You hear the birds? Think of what Jesus said about them. Hear that siren? Pray for any souls in distress.

Day 23: Hear the world's suffering. It can be overwhelming at times. But I'm reminded of how the women who stayed to the end, watching the crucifixion (how awful that must have been), were the first to see the empty tomb, that sign of the resurrection. When sadness and mourning interrupt your prayers, know that we worship one who suffered and suffers with us.

Day 24: Repeat your prayers. A concern, a need, a difficulty, a challenge can linger and force us to come back to God over and over again with the same desires, the same request. That's not bad. Persistence is everything. Be like the importunate widow in Jesus' parable (Luke 18:1–8). Stick with it. The asking is what brings us to this godly place again and again.

Day 25: Lose your life for God. "For those who want to save their life will lose it, and those who lose their life for my sake, and for the sake of the gospel, will save it," Jesus said (Mark 8:35 NRSV). Losing track of your agenda, your long list of things to do? Good. The list will be there when you're finished with this time. You're in the prayerful daily practice of losing yourself.

Day 26: Think about death. You didn't really want to, but death popped into your head. Your own death. The death of a loved one. The mortality we all face. Take this as an opportunity to make each day count, each day matter. "Make each day your masterpiece," said legendary basketball coach John Wooden. Facing your mortality is a gift to be found in prayer.

Day 27: Love the Lord your God. The first and greatest commandment: to love the Lord our God "with all your heart and with all your soul and with all your strength and with all your mind" (Luke 10:27). It's so simple and so great. How do you show someone your love? You spend time with them. You listen to them. You do what they say. You enjoy their presence, as you are doing with God.

Day 28: Don't give up. The pleasures of meditation and prayer are never over. Nor are the challenges. When and if you stumble into what is called the dark night of the soul, know that it's an opportunity, not a dead end. God will reveal what's beyond that dark night, the sunrise that's happening already. As you let go of what is finite, you uncover in prayer what is eternal.

Day 29: Tap a prayer. In your silence, with your eyes closed, you might try this. Using the fingers of one hand, tap at your heart, your free hand, a knee, your cheek. This cues you to external expressions of an inner prayer: to feel God's love (the heart), to find your strength (the hand), to let go (the knee), to forgive (turning the other cheek).

Day 30: Be bold. As the old expression goes, "Be bold, and mighty forces will come to your aid." Be bold in love, be bold in service, be bold in creativity, be bold in prayer. The impossible is only possible with God. That's what you're finding out. We are all co-laborers with God. And God can do the most for us when we step out in faith. Make that your prayer.

Snippets of Psalms to Turn To

Give ear to my words, O Lord; give heed to my sighing.
—Psalm 5:1 (NRSV)

Guard me as the apple of the eye; hide me in the shadow of your wings.
—Psalm 17:8 (NRSV)

You are a hiding place for me; you preserve me from trouble.
—Psalm 32:7 (NRSV)

As a deer longs for flowing streams, so my soul longs for you, O God.
—Psalm 42:1 (NRSV)

Be to me a rock of refuge, a strong fortress, to save me, for you are my rock and my fortress.
—Psalm 71:3 (NRSV)

Restore us, O God; let your face shine, that we may be saved.
—Psalm 80:3 (NRSV)

O sing to the Lord a new song; sing to the Lord, all the earth.
—Psalm 96:1 (NRSV)

Do not hide your face from me in the day of my distress.

—PSALM 102:2 (NRSV)

For your steadfast love is higher than the heavens, and your faithfulness reaches to the clouds.

—PSALM 108:4 (NRSV)

With the LORD on my side I do not fear. What can mortals do to me?

—PSALM 118:6 (NRSV)

Teach me, O LORD, the way of your statutes, and I will observe it to the end.

—PSALM 119:33 (NRSV)

I lift up my eyes to the hills—from where will my help come?

—PSALM 121:1 (NRSV)

Out of the depths I cry to you, O LORD. Lord, hear my voice!

—PSALM 130:1–2 (NRSV)

Your name, O LORD, endures forever, your renown, O LORD, throughout all ages.

—PSALM 135:13

Let everything that breathes praise the LORD! Praise the LORD!

—PSALM 150:6

Notes

PREFACE

1. Matthew Thorpe and Rachael Link, "12 Science-Based Benefits of Meditation," Healthline, last updated October 27, 2020, https://www.healthline.com/nutrition/12-benefits-of-meditation; Madhuleena Roy Chowdhury, "5 Health Benefits of Daily Meditation According to Science," PositivePsychology.com, May 23, 2021, https://positivepsychology.com/benefits-of-meditation.

CHAPTER 1: MEDITATION IN CHURCH?

1. Anonymous, *The Cloud of Unknowing with the Book of Privy Counsel*, trans. Carmen Acevedo Butcher (Boston: Shambhala, 2009).
2. Pew Research Center, "Religious Landscape Study," accessed September 14, 2021, https://www.pewforum.org/religious-landscape-study/.

CHAPTER 2: PICK A TIME AND A PLACE

1. Jill Jackson and Sy Miller, "Let There Be Peace on Earth," Jan-Lee Music, 1955.
2. Rick Hamlin, *10 Prayers You Can't Live Without: How to Talk to God About Anything* (Charleston, VA: Hampton Roads, 2016), xi.
3. Jean-Pierre de Caussade, *Abandonment to Divine Providence* (New York: Benziger Brothers, 1887), xx.
4. Caravaggio, *The Conversion of St. Paul* (also known as *The Conversion of Saul*), c. 1601, oil on canvas, 230 × 175 cm (Cerasi Chapel, Santa Maria del Popolo, Rome).

5. Rick Hamlin, *Finding God on the A Train: A Journey into Prayer* (San Francisco: HarperSanFrancisco, 1997).

CHAPTER 3: MEDITATE ON THE WORD

1. Anonymous, *The Cloud of Unknowing with the Book of Privy Counsel,* trans. Carmen Acevedo Butcher (Boston: Shambhala, 2009), 11.
2. Karle Wilson Baker, "Courage," *Poetry: A Magazine of Verse,* October 1921, https://www.poetryfoundation.org/poetrymagazine /browse?volume=19&issue=1#!/20573276.
3. Anonymous, *The Cloud of Unknowing,* 83–84.

CHAPTER 4: LISTEN TO YOUR ANGER

1. John of the Cross, letter 20 (to a Carmelite nun, 1590), in *The Collected Works of St. John of the Cross,* 3rd ed., trans. Kieran Kavanaugh and Otilio Rodriguez (Washington, DC: ICS Publications, 2017), 755.
2. Thomas Keating, *Invitation to Love: The Way of Christian Contemplation,* 20th anniv. ed. (New York: Bloomsbury, 2012), 105.
3. John of the Cross, "The Sayings of Light and Love," in *The Collected Works of St. John of the Cross,* 97.
4. Stephen Sondheim, "The Little Things You Do Together," *Company* (New York: Hal Leonard, 1970).
5. Parker Palmer's Thirteen Ways of Looking at Community," Center for Courage & Renewal, July 10, 2014, https:// couragerenewal.org/wpccr/13-ways-of-looking-at -community_parker-palmer/.

CHAPTER 5: HEAR THE WORRIES

1. Lawrence LeShan, *How to Meditate: A Guide to Self-Discovery* (Boston: Little, Brown 1974).

2. John Greanleaf Whittier, "Dear Lord and Father of Mankind," The Hymnal 1982: According to the Use of the Episcopal Church (New York: Church Publishing, 1985), 652, 653.

CHAPTER 6: JUST TRY PRAYING . . . AND YOU'LL BE DOING IT!

1. Alyson Shontell, "The Monk Scientists Call the 'World's Happiest Man' Reveals His Secret," *Independent*, January 28, 2016, https://www.independent.co.uk/life-style/health-and -families/features/monk-scientists-call-world-s-happiest-man -reveals-his-secret-a6839366.html.

2. Elliott Roosevelt and James Brough, *Mother R.: Eleanor Roosevelt's Untold Story* (New York: Putnam, 1977), 151.

3. David Michaelis, *Eleanor* (New York: Simon & Schuster, 2020).

4. Thomas Merton, *The Seven Storey Mountain* (New York: Harcourt Brace, 1948).

5. Robert Browning, "Andrea del Sarto," Poetry Foundation, https://www.poetryfoundation.org/poems/43745/andrea -del-sarto.

CHAPTER 7: FOCUS ON DEATH

1. *Los Angeles Times*, "Claire Townsend; Studio Executive, Attorney," December 21, 1995, https://www.latimes.com /archives/la-xpm-1995–12–21-mn-16552-story.html.

2. Claire Townsend, *The Spirit of Peace* directed by David Mueller (1995), film documentary.

3. The untitled cartoon by Roz Chast originally appeared in the October 25, 1993 edition of the *New Yorker*. It can be viewed at https://condenaststore.com/featured/new-yorker-october-25th -1993-roz-chast.html.

4. National Center for Health Statistics, "U.S. State Life Tables, 2018," Centers for Disease Control and Prevention, https://www .cdc.gov/nchs/nvss/life-expectancy.htm.

5. Father Horton, "St. Teresa of Ávila: 'If This Is How You Treat Your Friends . . . ,'" *Fauxtations* (blog), October 3, 2016, https://fauxtations.wordpress.com/2016/10/03/st-teresa-of-avila-if-this-is-how-you-treat-your-friends/.

6. Teresa of Ávila, *The Interior Castle*, ed. and trans. E. Allison Peers (Mineola, NY: Dover, 2012), 53.

7. Craig Impelman, "John Wooden's 7-Point Creed: 'Be True to Yourself,'" TheWoodenEffect.com, December 13, 2016.

CHAPTER 8: LOOK AT THE IMAGES IN YOUR HEAD

1. Giovanni Battista Moroni, *The Tailor (Il Sarto, or Il Tagliapanni)*, c. 1570, oil on canvas, 99.5 × 77 cm (The National Gallery, London), https://www.frick.org/exhibitions/moroni/23.

2. Giovanni Battista Moroni, *Portrait of Isotta Brembati Grumelli*, c. 1552, oil on canvas, 160 x 115 cm (National Museum in Warsaw, Warsaw, Poland).

3. Giovanni Battista Moroni, *Giovanni Gerolamo Grumelli (Il Cavaliere in Rosa, or The Man in Pink*, 1560, oil on canvas, 216 × 123 cm (Fondazione Museo di Palazzo Moroni, Bergamo), https://www.frick.org/exhibitions/moroni/35.

4. Giovanni Battista Moroni, *Two Donors in Adoration before the Madonna and Child and St. Michael*, c. 1557–60, oil on canvas, 89.5 × 97.8 cm (Virginia Museum of Fine Arts, Richmond), https://www.frick.org/exhibitions/moroni/6.

5. Hans Süss von Kulmbach, *The Ascension of Christ*, 1513, oil on fir, 61.5 × 38.1 cm. (Metropolitan Museum of Art, New York), https://www.metmuseum.org/art/collection/search/436835.

6. James William Kimball, *Encouragements to Faith* (London: Religious Tract Society, n.d.), 21.

7. Henry Ossawa Tanner Biography," Biography.com, April 2, 2014, https://www.biography.com/artist/henry-ossawa-tanner.

8. Henry Ossawa Tanner, *Nicodemus*, 1899, oil on canvas, 85.6 × 100.3 cm (Pennsylvania Academy of the Fine Arts, Philadelphia), https://www.pafa.org/museum/collection/item /nicodemus.

CHAPTER 9: PUT AWAY YOUR PHONE (EVERY NOW AND THEN)

1. Statista Research Department, "Average Time Spent Daily on a Smartphone in the United States 2021," March 25, 2021, https:// www.statista.com/statistics/1224510/time-spent-per-day-on -smartphone-us/.

CHAPTER 10: HOLD A GOOD THOUGHT FOR OTHERS

1. Thomas Traherne, *Centuries of Meditations*, ed. Bertram Dobell (London: Published by the editor, 1908), 124.

2. Traherne, 128.

3. Jay McCarl, "The One-Word Telegram," JayMcCarl.com, July 25, 2016, https://jaymccarl.com/2016/07/25/the-one-word-telegram/.

4. Traherne, *Centuries*, 120.

5. Traherne, 122.

6. "This Little Light of Mine," https://hymnary.org/text /this_little_light_of_mine_im_gonna_let.

7. Traherne, *Centuries*, 124.

8. Teresa of Ávila, *The Interior Castle*, ed. and trans. E. Allison Peers (Mineola, NY: Dover, 2012), 31.

9. Thomas Traherne, *Centuries*, 122.

CHAPTER 11: ACCEPT WHAT SEEMS IMPOSSIBLE TO ACCEPT

1. Catherine Marshall, "The Prayer of Relinquishment," *Guideposts*, January 7, 2015, https://www.guideposts.org /faith-and-prayer/prayer-stories/the-prayer-of-relinquishment.

2. Kulmbach, *The Ascension of Christ*, 1513, oil on fir, 61.5 × 38.1 cm. (Metropolitan Museum of Art, New York), https://www .metmuseum.org/art/collection/search/436835.

Chapter 12: Praise God from Whom All Blessings Flow

1. Carl Gustav Boberg, "How Great Thou Art," trans. by Stuart K. Hine, https://hymnary.org/text/o_lord_my_god_when_i_in _awesome_wonder.
2. Thomas Merton, *New Seeds of Contemplation* (New York: New Directions, 2007), 131.
3. Irving Berlin, "The Song Is Ended," 1927.
4. C. S. Lewis, *The Problem of Pain* (London: Centenary Press, 1940), 94.

About the
Author

A longtime editor at *Guideposts* magazine, *Rick Hamlin* is a frequent contributor to all Guideposts publications. He often writes about his prayer journey and has hosted numerous prayer events for the Guideposts community, in person and on social media. A busy husband, father, and lay leader in his church, he stresses how prayer and meditation can be a natural part of everyday life. He grew up in Southern California but has lived most of his adult life in New York City, where he and his wife sing in their church choir. In addition to his nonfiction—most recently *Pray for Me*—he has authored several novels, including *Reading Between the Lines*. Rick blogs regularly at guideposts.org and has published several op-eds in the *New York Times*.